GOD'S WORD

THE GUIDE FOR MANKIND

BILLY WILSON

Copyright © 2019 by Billy Wilson.

ISBN   Softcover   978-1-950580-92-7

All rights reserved. No part of this book may be reproduced or transmitted in any form or by any means, electronic or mechanical, including photocopying, recording, or by any information storage and retrieval system without express written permission from the author, except in the case of brief quotations embodied in critical reviews and certain other non-commercial uses permitted by copyright law.

Printed in the United States of America.

To order additional copies of this book, contact:
Bookwhip
1-855-339-3589
https://www.bookwhip.com

CONTENTS

Chapter 1   Words; God's Word 1

Chapter 2   Sex, a World Troubling Word: A People Motivator ... 23

Chapter 3   God's People Are Different 31

Chapter 4   God's Judgements Can Get Ruff and Permanent 45

CHAPTER 1

WORDS; GOD'S WORD

Everybody seems to be puzzled about what has and is happening to this world especially our country, America. The answer to any question is found in the King James Authorized Bible. People that have not learned to use the Bible as their guide have not learned much. Therefore, God has told his people to read and study in it continuously. Until one knows everything there is to know there is no danger in him reading too much from the Bible. Maybe misinterpreting it. God has told us how not to do that.

One will find no help from the spiritual world in anything else above that. It is Jesus Christ himself and is all Truth, the Whole Truth, nothing but the Truth. This Country used to swear to these Words with their hand on the Bible and ending with the words: *So, help me God*, for anything official. Our founding fathers would not recognize our approach to legal matters today. People have a dislike for having to tell the truth and have changed their commitment to such thinking.

God has said, "If one does not believe ever Word he has given to us about his Son," We are none of his. The Bible is his Son. Nothing in the Bible any plainer than that to one that will study and believe it.

As we look upon this country today, with almost every day's hideous crimes and bloodshed plus filled with natural disasters; that we are not accustom to seeing all around us with no reasoning about them and all indications are it is getting and going to keep getting much worse. We need to face the truth and confess a few things to ourselves and assume a deeper investigation into how we got that way. It has taken several years for us to drift into this bad a shape, with our wrong teaching and lack of any decent teaching at all until it is hardly safe to walk into the streets. Any country that is forgetting God, is drifting into confusion and oblivion.

If we would read and believe the *Bible*, one could see it is God himself, all the truth and help we have here on this earth. That can never be found anywhere else, it is the only book on earth that is Spiritually written and spiritually discerned, and not one word in it can ever be changed.

If it could it would not be God's Word any more, it has been sealed for over one thousand years. Why Satan's people hate it so, they are nothing but liars and can never be anything else. The Bible has pronounced the death sentence on all of them. The reason why Satan's people have wared against it and swore to do away with it at any cost. They have not destroyed one page in it yet, and never will.

It will take just as long and maybe harder to teach us back into enough decency until we can see the difference. It will take much work from the generation that is at hand unto the generation that is coming on. As this generation of schools and parents *are* the problem, they will have to be taught something first. It is for sure our government will not do anything about this since they are the ones that are doing the teaching, leading us into where we are at. Coming from Mystery Babylon there at Rome and we do not seem to have enough sense to know it. *If a country wants to survive it must seek God. He is the provider.*

If one has not studied the Bible he may not have heard the name, *Mystery Babylon*. John had not heard it until an Angel spoke to him in heaven, it must be a heavenly word. Only mentioned one time in the Bible but the whole Bible is written around and about it and we are rolling into it. Ready or not, mostly not, for the world hardly knows what it is. Talk about being so deep in the forest until one cannot see the trees!!

The Bible teaches we must have a revolution to break out of it, but we have no place to seek one from or to. We have no country to furnish us more people like the Pilgrims and Puritans to do the job, other countries are in just as bad shape as we are. That means it will have to come from within.

We will have to have an uprising, something like the uprising of God haters that we have going on now, but on the other side of things; starting in our schools called Mystery Babylon where most all our teaching originates from. The women are seeking an uprising position, with their marches and such, maybe they will save us. God warns us they will rule over us in end times but will be our downfall.

I can guarantee we will have to use every method available, to win the battle. We might figure out what God meant when he instructed his people to fight and put the enemy *out* from among us. Our schools are the biggest enemy and problems this country has. False teaching is the biggest enemy among us. That does not imply to kill the children, but we must contain them and control them back to their God given rights or order, to be taught and raised in the fear and admonition of the Lord Jesus Christ, the only correct way. If our teachers do not have it, they can never teach our children to have it.

This country was built and blessed in accordance with what God has promised to any people that would believe and adhere to his Word, which is the King James Translation of the Bible. We attained the Bible without any help from the Mystery Babylon Schools. If mothers taught our children in our homes as God told us to. Our schools should be nothing more or less than just an extension of our Christion Holmes, the way it started out being, with the Bible being all of its foundation and basics.

As we have been getting farther away from the Bible, we have been getting more and more of what God plainly promised to any people that would dare to forget or ignore him our try to bypass him. Which is impossible to do as we should see by now.

I can remember seeing much of this happening as I am now seventy- eight years old. The beginning of the change started much farther back than I have seen but I have saw much of the big changing as it was getting so, big, successful, and prominent.

It was in the very late nineteen-hundred-and forties and early fifties. Probably one of the biggest licks was when they give us the great consolidation of the school systems when all the schools started obtaining school busses and complete government control. They were so handy in taking the children from their homes, churches and families. They started many drastic changes of about everything concerning our education. Mainly throwing the Bible out; one cannot teach the creation without the Bible, and making mankind his own creator.

The government was taking complete charge of our children. Some of it was good and some not so good. Some parents were proud to give up their children, some were a little reluctant, but none of them was given any choice. Now they belong to Mystery Babylon of Rome. Everything happened a little at a time but moved along rapidly and ending up with some very drastic results.

A few examples: if the government did not approve of the way a home was educating its children they could just pick them up and place them in another home and parents. Even when it had nothing to do with the child's character learning, government can bus them to any place for schooling they desire to send them; just for their conveniences or to accomplish their demands; is that not owning the children?? Which sometimes are radical and untrue. Such as, there is no such thing as a God and creator, that would crowd mankind and parents completely out of the picture.

How close are the crimes in children from old schools, to the ones who have had schooling from the government today? I believe they were much less crime and much easier to handle.

Christians? Show me where the Bible gave responsibility of our children to any carnal government anywhere in it! The Bible, or from the Bible, is a Christian's only school book needed. One can never learn all of it not to mention how it is to be applied. It is big enough to test every child or parent of any school. I am fully aware of the drastic effort it would be to bring about such a change. How long did it take to perfect the system we have now, no God and no church allowed?

Schools started out in the church houses, at the start the Bible and God was the center of the entire schooling system. I remember the day I did not see a school teacher but what had a Bible on or in their desk. It was well understood to be the judge and guide to settle all disagreements and doctoring. Most of the teachers kept a hefty little stick they called a pointer-stick they could point things out over all the blackboards and could back up the Bible with it very well.

I could tell some good stories about the big-boys learning to respect the set-up, and they usually did. I do not recall one child getting any health damage from any school discipline, but I have seen many of them whipped, received a few of them myself. Did not hurt my health any.

The education department that was formed by the government was completely carnal and could not in no way teach their carnality from a Spiritually Written Book. Causing a conflict that is getting worse and worse and is going on until today still getting worse. Until the government has outlawed the Bible from the schools they used to belong to.

The Bible and the people belong to the schools, but the government could not follow them. Mystery Babylon from Rome could not compete with the Bible it was just too true, they could not teach their lies from it. They have now taken over our complete country, government, and everything else, by taking over our schools. The mention of Christ is outlawed. The government that used to be of the people, now owns the people. They told us around three-hundred years ago just how they were going to do it and did it.

Schools are not the only thing the government has took completely over, there is about nothing private to a citizen anymore. We can own land and build houses but must pay payments on them to the government in the form of taxes and insurance that gets higher every day on everything we own. If you do not the Government will move you out in the street and take everything you own.

Like I have written, some of this is good and some is not so good, but when the people have lost all control of any of the government through lies and false promises, very little of this looks good at all.

Even after we defeated the Devil's in two world wars and I do not know how many other smaller wars to gain our independence and be free to worship any God as we chose to. Seems our forefathers fought and died for our freedom all in vain. We have let foreign, God-hating, America hating, illegal aliens flood over our borders demanding we feed, pay their hospital bills, educate them, and preach to us that is what our God says for us to do. They tell us they know him better than we do, and we believe them. But they can hold on to that only if they can destroy our Bibles.

It seems like any man that can read any in the Bible and look around could see that is plainly the shape we are in today just exactly as God warned us. The Bible will answer every question, that is why evil men hate it and dedicated to destroying and replacing it with such stupid things, as an older Bible, or a stupid man-written Bible that is so much smarter than God.

There is no such thing as a Bible written by Jesus Christ other than the King James Translation. Christians are named after Christ, he told us the Bible is him, he wrote it and does not want one word in it adjusted. Seems we have never been told that or just cannot believe it. To not believe it sends one to hell, as a non-believer.

All other writings on the face of the earth was considered and covered in the King James Bible written by Jesus in around 1600 AD. After England sought God to give them a word to lead them correctly and pleasing to God and end the confusion that was getting God's people killed from the earth. He did and since that happening no man, with a clear unselfish mind, will not be speaking against the Word of God. That man cannot belong to God.

Men will climb trees to get to believe a lie when he could stand on the ground and believe the truth and be blessed of God. Easy way to tell the character of a person. I have been trying for over forty years to get somebody to explain such men to me. Having a hatred for God who is nothing but Truth, and a love for his adversary, the Devil which is nothing but lies. God calls it believing a lie and being dammed. God says he will send great delusion to them that will not believe the truth.

I am sure our founding fathers could quickly give us some good advice. The first thing they would notice would be the drastic hole we have created by throwing God out of our country that Truth built for us. Of course, they would not be familiar with Mystery Babylon overseeing everything, they fought hard and suffered many things ridding themselves of that yoke and rope. To be able to freely worship God, and all the country's *people* to be represented instead of only illegal foreigners and Christ haters and criminals. These are all the Devil's people can recognize.

I was told by my grade school teacher that George Washington, in his farewell address, said that this country should never make any binding treaties with Europe. It was puzzling to me at the time, I did not understand. I do not believe I have heard it again in the seventy years since. Think about it, Washington had more foresight and common sense in his cold dead body when they were burying him than all of our teachers and leaders today could muster up among themselves. We have gone steadily downhill ever since they got him buried, until we are convinced we could not exist without them binding treaties with Europe. It is Europe that could not exist.

God has warned us we are a blessed and superior race of people than the Devil's people. But the Devil that is teaching us now is making us ashamed of it and telling us we must become inferior and below his people to belong to God. I do not remember reading that in my Bible.

It is easy to tell the enemies and haters of this great country, just look at our *trained school teachers and politicians*. They are not trained in or from God's Word any more. They are constantly being bitter and making as much trouble and racket against everything and everybody that is doing the least thing for God or their neighbor and this great country. As I say often, it does not make any sense to a person with an ounce of godly sense and a sound mind. I reckon we do not have a thread of either one any more. Our teachers certainly do not.

Satan has them at his step and our children at their step, and Godly men at the children's step. Strange how easy our parents and school teachers can raise an entire generation of such God hating people. They must be completely taken in and possessed by the Devil himself. I see no hope for any such people or the children they raise, therefore no hope for our country. This country is not safe for God friendly people any longer, they are the Devil's worst enemy. One would think with over twenty-trillion dollars in the hole and cannot feel safe to set in a house of worship, we could have paid the world into a little more prosperity walking than it is showing. Read your Bible one can find out why.

If God's people do not wake up and fight for our rights as the people did that settled and built this country in the starting. It will soon be doomed to become one of the lowest nations left on the globe. If they cannot establish their arguments with two or three witnesses from the Bible that Jesus said he wrote then they are lying. We are told of God, to not allow them into one's house, and to not give them God speed, no, not to eat with them and to put them out from among ourselves. God's people cannot do any of that any more, since we have given up everything we ever Spiritually Owned. If one believes in God, he believes in the Spirit.

Jesus named his people an army that would stand and fight and would prevail over the world If they would separate themselves from the world. Not join them and fight both sides from the middle of them. Even his disciples won nothing that way, and they did not have a King James Bible and did not fight; just preached. Fighting would have won them nothing, but their life's sacrifices won us the greatest country ever has been. We are told to fight to hang onto it. God is still with us as long as we protect the Jews, but we are turning from them and God is going to turn from us when we do. Anybody working for Satan hates the Jews. If one hates the Jews, one is working for Satan.

If we cannot win a battle in our country, how do we expect to go abroad and win other countries. The only country I read about John the Beloved going off to was Patmos and Heaven, he did more work for Jesus towards end-times than all the other disciples put together, the only one that was not killed by Satan. He lived to be maybe sixty years older than any of the other disciples. History tells us he lived to be over one hundred years old and died at the church at Ephesus.

Maybe we should study how he got off the Isle of Patmos to do that. Jesus would not let them kill him although he suffered many things. Even sent to the Rock of Patmos, which was a death sentence, so him and John could be alone, and Jesus could give to him the book of Revelation. It does not say how he got back to the churches, but history tells us he did and lived to be maybe a hundred and ten years old.

We are not being treated unfairly but spoiled ourselves until we think we have gotten ahead of God. The people of this country threw out the things we used to worship and thank God for. I Guess they were too heavy for them to carry, slowing down their speed too much. Where were they going? I have never saw a Bible that was that heavy.

After all the things God has done for this country, we have chosen our government as our God and to teach and raise our children which is all carnally based. We have let the government outlaw God from our schools and forbid our Military Chaplains to say the name of Jesus while in a uniform. The Bible cannot be carried onto government property.

God has said he is a jealous God, and nothing is to sit in his seat but the Word of God. We chose to govern ourselves and threw God's Word out. This was why the Pilgrims came to this country, to have freedom to worship God. Money and power from greedy men from Mystery Babylon have bought it out for the Devil.

God did not find a man that could stand up to this world to lead this country back to God until he raised up trump. A man that we did not deserve. Some of our so-called Christians are trying to kill him off. I have news for them, Trump is not going until God is through with him and them trying to kill him, are not Christians. Then woe unto the ones that *gets* it done. If it is the whole country, then woe unto the whole country. One that so choses, can crawl under the porch and watch it happening.

We took the attitude that somebody owes us all these things, for our good looks I guess. We have forgotten that this country was formed as One Nation Under God. We have "*In God we Trust*" written on all our federal pieces of money and every coin and legal tender note. We have Godly quotes written, on or in, maybe every shrine in Washington D. C, because to our founding fathers they are very true. They were not put there by this Antichrist hell-bent generation we have now that is tearing them all down.

As a matter of fact, thinking them to be offensive to our modern intelligence is the reason they are being tore down. Our country cannot stand much more of our modern intelligence and stay in existence or have independence for anybody, but godless foreigners and Devil-possessed American-hating Liberal Democrats, some of the greediest people in the world that God is turning lose on us. They want them for they will all vote Liberal Democrat. I say they are all welcome to go to hell if that is what they want, but I prefer to stay with God the creator.

Our country has grown into blaspheming, cursing, and blaming God instead of honoring him. God says that is a death sentence, even unto the second death in hell. And we are wandering why we are not blessed as we used to be and owe more than twenty-three trillion dollars. God will not honor any such country as we have become but has promised poverty and destruction to it. (Ask California that is burning, washing and killing itself off the map) Provided to us by *Mystery Babylon*, a name from God himself. Only seen one time in the scriptures but much of the Bible referring to and around it. From the beginning to the very end, God, is the only one to have salvation.

Over twenty-three trillion dollars in debt with all the other miserable things, should be enough to convince anybody God meant what he said. Such as the floods, drafts, earth-quicks, border invasions, storms and fires; our young kids killing one another. People killing one another and anybody else that gets in their way, for no reason. They just have not received any decent moral teaching to stand up for or with. That is not the way our Bible teaches us to stand and fight for Truth and for the rights God gave to us.

I am looking for Mystery Babylon to have us tearing all that antique stuff down any day, *things that relates to God or our founding forefathers.* And they will as soon as the Mystery Babylon Whore and the Antichrist Muslims take over, and they are going too. This is in the process of happening at this time. After we have fought at least three wars with them and won ours and England's independence, but we don't seem to be able to hold onto it.

They have already torn down and outlawed and rewritten our history.

Too much God in it for them and most of our, so called, Christians are content with the government from Rome that does not know God, running us, becoming our God and telling us to except it. Who are they working for, themselves, or the Devil's government? Seems one with any intelligence should know the answer to that is, *both of them.*

The <u>Mystery Babylon Pope</u> (God calls the False Prophet) has lately come up with a suggestion to change a word in the Bible, testing the waters and hoping someone might pick up on it. It has never been done since the testators that wrote it has died over a thousand years ago. It has never seen a word changed in it, and never will see it. Meaning the contents of the original of it are sealed. Jesus has blocked them from changing a word in it. If they do it is not Jesus' Word any more nor the Original King James Authorize Version. It would be an altered copy and under another name and would be of none Spiritual effect to God's people.

It would be a Big-Feather in the pope's hat to accomplish such a feat or even get someone started to get interested in it. It could open the gate for others in the near future. The Devil and the Pope are working together.

The Antichrist has not come on the scene yet but will and is trying to work its way in now; the Ten Kings of the Middle East are at hand.

I wonder why the Pope cares about what is in the Bible, he doesn't believe or use it and has been trying to kill all the Christians and bury it since it was written. They do not believe in the Holy Spirit of God (Bible), for the Bible sends them to hell. If I were them I would be worrying too. Their church is called Mystery Babylon (God's name for it) in the book of Revelations. Keep reading and find what the word Babel stands for and has grown into.

In the beginning, everything in the world spoke the same language. After the flood people got a big idea and started to organize into one and build a tower against God thinking nobody could flood nor bother them again. God was not worried that man was going to get bigger than him; but knew if they could organize into *one* that well and build a stand against him, they would never be one man saved from the earth. They would always be serving self. God shortened their life span for the sake of man.

God came down and confused their language from the earth to scatter them. They came to work next morning, and no one could understand his neighbor. They sounded to one another like babbling, thus began the first word of the Babylon Language; "Babel."

They had to separate into small groups and each group had to learn a new language in order to communicate with each other. They have been scattering to the four winds of the world ever since. Nations are settled around their language holding them together until today. The place where they started the tower called Babel, thus Babylon, means a *name* for a town, city, community, or gathering place for people into one, was invented. America is trying to beat the system and divide into *everybody's* language not knowing that was for a purpose to divide. Of course, America is smarter than God, are they not sitting in his seat? Each person has his own language and unable to organize into one. Every carnal language is a Babylon, except the King James Bible, it is excepted of God. Only the words that are in it, any other word is a carnal word.

In the spirit from the Bible, Babylon is a word used for the seven-headed Beast Riders on one beast throughout the Bible. Started from the word Babel that was given to the place of the tower and settlement in the beautiful valley they had quit moving and settled in. It is carried today as a name for a similar place, where people stopped moving, organized into one and grew into a lasting *place* in the Bible; like Babylon.

Like the seven headed beast kingdoms, first Egypt, then Canaan, then the third beast head that was named Babylon, the fourth Medes Persia, the fifth Greece. The sixth Rome, the seventh Rome with ten kings that had receive no kingdom as yet added to it. God, from heaven added the word *Mystery* onto <u>*Babylon,*</u> in the book of Revelation being built onto Babel as John was looking from heaven at the biggest conglomeration of people and governments ever been put together as one, since the beginning of time, thus a Mysterious settlement.

It has become the greatest Christian and Jew slaying machine on earth since they crucified Christ outside Jerusalem, starting point of our A.D. Calendar. They killed over a hundred-million Christians and Jews in the first thousand-years after killing Christ. Why Jesus named them as being drunk on the blood of the saints when naming them in the seventeenth chapter of Revelations. They are now enjoying the biggest religious organization in the world and do not except the Spirit of God as being on this earth. God is a spirit and they sure do not know him.

Mystery Babylon has never been known as a beast but a beast rider. They will be seen riding on the biggest beast of the world if not they will be trying to. God gave the Bible to England around sixteen-hundred AD after them sincerely seeking him for it, making England the most powerful nation on earth. Ruled over every continent on the earth and the seas and was blessed from every direction it could look.

Until they turned their salvation over to the False Prophet Church there at Rome claiming to be the very vicar of the Christ that they killed. Then started persecuting and killing anybody and everybody that would not worship their so-called Pope. How can they, or anybody that knows Jesus Christ, believe Jesus will save them after he called them, "MYSTERY BABYLON THE GREAT, THE MOTHER OF HARLOTS AND ABOMATIONS OF THE EARTH;" Revelations, Seventeenth Chapter; Much more he did say about them. Like being drunk on the blood of the Saints and Martyrs of Christ.

The Spirit is Jesus Christ, Mystery Babylon does not think they need him. True Christians will never believe any such a lie as they are telling themselves and others. The Bible tells us of how Jesus will throw all of Mystery Babylon into the lake of fire with every soul whose name is not written down in the Book of Life at the end of the millennial reign. The end of that story and the end of the old heaven and earth, covered completely in the twentieth chapter of Revelations.

Babylon the Beast moved to Medes Persia for its fourth head's location then to Greece for its fifth head. Later it moved to Rome for its sixth head, which went into perdition, for its seventh head's location. With God it is still Babylon the seven headed beast that so much of the Bible is about and around. Each head had a name given to it but the same beast. Was rolled into hell at the end with every soul that had not its name written down in the book of life. I believe that is the largest number of souls ever written. God simply referred to them as the number of the sands on the seashores. We had no name then for a number that big. And still don't have.

The Bible *is* the Holy Spirit and *is* Jesus himself. I can see why they forbid their people to have a Bible and forbidding us to have one in our schools and trying to exclude Jesus from our conversations and military services. The Bible is Jesus Christ and they will not except him for he is the head of his people. And they think they are the only head anywhere they are at. Common sense should know Jesus did not write and give us the Bible for us to judge God with, but the Pope seems to think he did.

Anybody should know his suggestion to change one word in the Bible, is just a fishing-ploy for them to try and kill the Christian Religion, which is the Bible. This is just the way Satan works; a little step at a time but never misses an opportunity. I would vote that he is the one that needs to go. They killed Christ and have been trying to kill his influence ever since.

Many millions of people have died to protect that Book which is Jesus Christ, most of them by the hands of Mystery Babylon, which is the Pope or Father of all the souls whose names are not written down in the Lamb's Book of Life. He is called the <u>World's Holy Father</u>. I believe a few more are left ready to separate from them even if it means death, but that does not include many of the hypocritical Christians of today, just the ones that loves Jesus, the Bible.

The names have continued to move and grow, but I believe all of them are man's names added onto God's name. That was John looking at the sum of them making up Mystery Babylon as the angel in heaven had named it. The Antichrist (The incoming ten kings) is to burn Rome the city from the earth while the world watches; God's doings after he calls his people out.

Rome, the city, is burned from the earth but the sixth head only goes into the seventh head with ten horns and completely teamed with the Antichrist and its Ten Muslims Kings. Gone is the city Rome and anyone that might have been Christians. The Muslims could not stand the evidence of where the so-called Christians were headquartered at for so long. So, they burned the city from the earth, God's doings, after he calls his people out of it. This battle will go on until Christ intervenes to save some flesh on the earth. The remaining people will be known as the Antichrist.

We that have read the Bible know the battle that is coming, and we need to fight to save as much of America as we can. God has referred to us as an army and has told us (America, about the only Christian nation) to fight for Truth (Which is Jesus). America's people are to be prepared for Jesus to gather them up at the twinkling of an eye. It will save us, and it will help our children that are coming along after us to recognize the builder of nations and be prepared for him to come back or appear.

We need to teach and prepare them as much as we can, instead of giving them over to a Pope and joining the world to fight both ways from the middle of them. The Antichrist Muslim's Ten Kings that are destined to rule the world and vowed to eliminate the Christians and Mystery Babylon with them. These Battles of the end times that are spoken of in God's Word are fought between Mystery Babylon and the ten Muslim Antichrist Kingdoms that are just now showing up on the world stage. They have each killed several hundred million Christians and Jews since Christ was born. Hitler, perhaps being the chief killer among them; so far.

Why Jesus gave the description of them as being drunk on the blood of the saints which I do not believe we have seen a comparison yet. The Pope represents Mystery Babylon; the Muslims represents the Antichrist, God's name for them. They will unite and war for some time, God not on either side, giving Christians some space in between, until the people will become in danger of being annihilated from the earth if Christ does not intervene.

Israel will be the only country to protect the Christians along about that time, the Christians and Jews will be one people and be with Christ at Armageddon. Located in the hills around Jerusalem. None of God's people should be a hater of the Jews, as so many are today. You might end up friendless, claiming Christianity and hating Jews. God says, the time is coming when all nations will turn against God's people, the Jews. Them nations will not be Christians, Jesus is a Jew and not ashamed of it. But will be ashamed of them who are.

God's people are the only ones that can save the Bible and our country. And they are the only thing that can save themselves from the Devil- Possessed world God calls, "The Antichrist" that is just starting to make his play on the earth. We cannot do anything without God's help, and we will not get God's help without believing, seeking and receiving him. The Bible is Jesus Christ and he is a Jew. He will never turn against his people that will turn to him instead of taking the Mark of the Beast.

I have just been listening to the TV telling about another unbelievable school shooting with seventeen dead at this count. All the condolences and sympathy being showed to the victims over and over and all the questions being ask as to what has gone wrong with people today. Their answers are about to become wore out like God has said they would, and I can see no real help in any one of them I have heard. The answer is always Christ and I have never heard him named.

I am a preacher of the Gospel for forty years, and a very normal human being, I have been studying for the answers for anybody that might want to hear them. You can find every answer in God's Word, usually in several places. One place God says, man without God is a beast (animal) and anybody that denies his Spirit is without God. He is The Spirit.

It will not be easy to turn things back around into the Spirit. We have let the spirit of Satan take charge of this entire country. I have been writing about it in I believe every one of my books, for the past five years. There are eight of them published at this time and can be bought anywhere books are sold. Allow me to take another stab at it, if you do not love the Lord you will probably not like them.

I have been preaching hard that this country was led into the Civil War by a bunch of Devil-possessed Liberals that was using the Devil's favorite slogan, _**DIVIDE AND CONQURE,**_ for their own selfish benefit. The very ground floor of the Liberals of today. They succeeded in tearing this country in two, close to the middle, trying to take control of their half. It would have been the death of the Union just like the world predicted would happen when this country started being established.

They told us there was no way that this many states and people could be held together without a Tyranny Government and a huge army. At that time, we were a one nation under-God country and set up in every way by God's Word, that made the difference. We still believed in God at that time and after much death and destruction during the Civil war, God let them get their differences and many wrongs, like slavery, out of their system. Held them together with one of the Godliest presidents maybe we ever had. He never gave up the cry to, "S*ave the union*".

With God's help he freed the slaves put the country back together with laws that all men were free and should be treated equal. In much better shape than when they started the war. I believe we can give God the credit for that and Lincoln's constant calling out to him in much prayer.

The Devil is trying the same old thing again with the so-called Liberal Christians solidly behind him. The Bible (Jesus Christ) is the only thing that has held us together. I have been told all my life, if one does not study history he will repeat the same mistakes over, and over. The Bible is the most correct and completed history book ever written. It holds the past, present, and future, in one book.

God has given us maybe the strongest and Godliest man he had available for a president. God puts them in there, we the people do not elect them. He gave us Obama to let us, we the people, see where our God haters would lead us. Then he gave us trump, we are trying to eliminate him. He is not perfect but handling the many big jobs without the people's help. Can you imagine what he could do with the people's help? What we better wake up and see is, God is helping Trump and he is not leaving until God is through with him. Them God hating Liberals will just have to cry in their milk. God is still in control.

How many Christians can you find supporting him? I guarantee you the ones that know God are but that is very few. How many times can you point to that Trump has spoken or acted against the Word of God or the Godly freedom of this country? I have hardly heard him make a speech without him referring to God somewhere in it.

What country's problem has he not improved upon? Yet the so-called Christians hate him. God will not forget that, he has a long memory and he does have an end to his patience.

Give me one reason why a Christion that loves our country or God should hate Trump. I would be interested in hearing it.

God has never told us to take care of the Devil's people of the world, they are about one-hundred per-cent of Trumps troubles. That is the Devil telling us them lies directly from the Liberal Democrats, determined to drag us down to his level. This country is falling for it wholesale. Anybody should see which one we are listening to, God or the Devil. The problem in all the school killings, the church killings, the law officer killings, are an in-the-mind thing. I did not say that to down-play the significance of one thing, but to show the great significance the mind plays in everything about us, including what we do.

Anything a person wanting to give to another person like an education, character, up-bringing, knowledge, attitude toward things of the world. You need to know and realize you are going to start by having to work with one's mind. And one needs to know a few things about the mind. As everybody's mind works a little different, but there are a few things that are alike in all minds. The mind must be dealing with the spiritual side of a person. It is not a carnal part that a carnal eye can see, only the evidence.

I doubt if any project has been started or finished without first being started in someone's mind. So, when we are looking for the cause of the killings and so many other unreasonable things, that are going on and are getting bigger. Maybe we should start looking at the mind-set of the humans that are involved and causing such things to happen. Especially our school teachers. And don't come at me with, it is impossible to know the mind of people.

That is just a lame-duck excuse for someone who does not want to listen to the truth. Ignore and excuse the truth is something God's people have done for much too long. Jesus is the Truth. You ask somebody about something, his first thought is *what is in this for me?* God does not need that kind of person. He is not going to bless or claim them kind of people.

That person is only interested in himself, and only looking out for self-first and that is not what God has told us to do. He told us to put self to death and put *him* first, then his people next, then one can take care of self with everything being for the good of God first. Killing Self was the title of my first book, can be ordered anywhere books are sold. If a thing cannot come through God's hands first, his blessing will never be with it; but only what that man that is for self-first can put upon it and you will have to depend upon sharing his leftovers. Is not that like being a beggar, taking his leftovers?

God says to put that kind of people out from among you. He will be having you at his step and that will not be for God first, then you would be stepping downward and that is where our people are going. Our nation has been going along with that to the tune of above ten trillion dollars in the last eight years. How long can we last at that rate? The interest is more than we can afford. The lying, left, liberals are telling us we are gaining and getting better off with them. One should see without any Mystery Babylon's schooling that these people (mostly Democrat TV broadcasters) are lying. No wonder God has said we are deaf and blind.

The ten Antichrist Kingdoms (*The Muslims*) are rising in the East to join and take charge of the Church there at Rome that God calls *Mystery Babylon, drunk on the blood of the saints*, the biggest Christian slaying thing in the world while claiming to be all the people's God. Killing six million Jews just while warming up for two world wars. God is going to burn their city, *Rome*, off the earth, God's doings. He has told us all about it in his Word. Read this; then when you see it happening you can remember you were told.

The Muslims will join the Mystery Babylon church and then burn their city from the earth and become the one God calls the Antichrist, and for a short time will rule the earth and try to kill the rest of the Christians and Jews. That statement is what most people are about, but it will not have a very good ending. Unless one is blind he can see it shaping up and starting into happening now. God will gather his elect from the four winds from one end of heaven to the other and take them to a place called Armageddon as he told about there in the twenty-fourth chapter of Matthew and explained in Revelations: Chapter Seventeen.

He will warn his people to come out of Mystery Babylon before he allows it to be burnt down. Odd! I have never heard that preached. You can read that in Revelations, seventeenth and eighteenth chapters, if one can get somebody to tell one how to read the Bible. It is an amazing book. God tells us *everything* in it, some of it thousands of years before it is to happen. Jesus Christ himself is the Spirit of Prophecy.

The Bible is Jesus Christ, there has never been another book like it in the world. There has never been another man like Jesus Christ. Have you ever known a man that could prophesy even in the same field with Jesus Christ? A huge Book covering over thousands of years and history of the creation and of all mankind from beginning to the end and not one word in it found to be false. That sounds to be unbelievable to anybody's mind, but one can look around himself, check thousands of years and find no mistake.

Anytime one thinks he has found a wrong statement in the King James Bible, he had better be prepared to be corrected. For it is him that will get it; it will never be the Bible. It is Jesus himself, he cannot ever be wrong.

The Bible is forever copyrighted in heaven in the name of Jesus Christ and can never be changed. If it is changed, it will not be the Bible in Jesus' name, and cannot be applied as such. God's people are always subjected to God's laws and will be treated as such and should treat each other as such. If one cannot see Jesus Christ, he will never see this fact.

It is binding to belong to the Lord Jesus Christ, the reason we should keep him on our minds day and night to not violate any of his laws. If we do, we should be ready to immediately repent and ask for mercy. God is not there to *get* you, but there to forgive and help you.

He always understands, and one can never deceive him. He knows everything, and we ought to know some things, like always keep him in our hearts. And if we will learn to look to, love and depend upon him he will prove himself to us over and over. But he is not in the habit of people telling him what and how to do things. Why should he when he knows everything about anything, we just need to learn to trust him.

He is the very air we breathe, the life that is in us. He is that close to us. If one does not know him, do not miss the chance to get to know him. We are considered dead without him. His Spirit is the only life in anything that has life in it.

CHAPTER 2

SEX, A WORLD TROUBLING WORD: A PEOPLE MOTIVATOR

When Jesus gave us the written King James Bible that he wrote in around sixteen hundred AD. He said he did not want a word in it changed or a word added to it. He spoke a lot about every sex, but he did not use the word, sex, in the entire Bible, making it a carnal word. Reckon he did not know how to spell it? He knew how to spell the words, fornication, adultery, unclean, lust, prostitutes, whoredoms, and I found nothing good he said about any of them but identified them all very plainly. Seems every one of them are related to sex.

Sex, one of the most powerful moving forces in the world among mankind was given to humans for reproduction purposes. God said to multiply and fill the earth. It is contrary to God and dangerous to use it for anything else or out of marriage. In *that*, the Muslims are far ahead of us. Maybe in an ungodly way, but still ahead. They are taking advantage of that being a weak side to our complete country, which they are determined to take over in any and every way they can.

God has warned us our women will rise up and rule over us in the last days. And they *will*, for a short time near the end. They are working in a Devil's world with a Devil's way and with his help.

They do not mind killing their own people that will not cooperate with their beliefs, and Christians cannot do that, just for that reason.

But I do believe in self-defense for me and mine, God has said to put them to death. I believe that is meant to mean when it is necessary to accomplish what he told us to do, like put them out from among yourselves.

God says Jesus is coming back or all flesh would be destroyed, the world is turning into a solid rage, read your Bible, we have been told everything.

I have been saying since I was just a kid and have never been meaning for it to sound smart, just true. When someone would comment on how bad things were getting, I would say, "You have not seen anything yet; just wait a while, I am guaranteed it is going to get worse." Sex has no earthly strength and value in running a country, or winning a war, just producing and motivating the people. It will get attention and steer up activity in almost any situation.

I have known people that believed money and sex was the only thing worth living for and said so. They had no moral values, and no Spiritual Knowledge, they have been taught carnally from our Mystery Babylon Schools and the world. No Christian-raising at all, Mystery Babylon will not allow it, they are completely carnal. If one teaches a God besides them, they are taken out of any control situation, or probably beheaded.

Carnal is, "Anything apart from the Spirit." The whole world, and now our country, has been pushed over the cliff with such carnal teachings as theirs. Like there is no such thing as a spirit they cannot produce or control. That leaves too many questions one cannot answer for me to buy into that. Although they are producing electronic controlled human bodies. They just have not put us in them as yet; but it is coming.

Like no reasoning, no consideration, no Constitution, no freedom of speech, no God except government, certainly not a Bible; is what our Mystery Babylon Government Schools are teaching and preparing our children for. It is called, "*Political Correctness*", which just means politicians are the only thing that is correct. This is to replace our Bible. Why would one need a Bible to serve a politician? They are the most God hating people on the planet. I don't know why God suffers them to live.

They or the devil's people, in a devil's world. God gave the choice to the people and we are sleeping in it. We have enough of them in and out of Washington DC they should win the war for us if they would put on a uniform and carry a gun against our enemies. But I would be afraid to arm them, they are God haters and for sure our country's worst enemies. They cannot touch God but can kill and persecute his people and do. God has warned us they would and to not let them set in God's seat. Nothing is to sit there but God's Word, our biggest problem on this earth is us tolerating and obeying them instead of God.

Our teaching, coming from the Mystery Babylon Schools that have taken over our schools and everything else in this country after losing two world wars to us. And I do not know how many smaller wars. They have lost every war to us until we turned from God. They have never been on our side. They manage to come out riding the beast that wins. Why God said they are not a beast, but a beast rider.

Most of us today do not know why we fought them but it was over being able to *worship God any way we please.* Now we can hardly worship him at all since we are taken over by Mystery Babylon from Rome, and not by wars. But by surrendering to their teaching. Our Christians or not believing God anymore, Rome is teaching us. I do not believe I have seen the words "Mystery Babylon" written in a carnal book. That should tell you how much the world knows about Mystery Babylon; not one thing.

Worship is defined as giving honor and glory to something, I am afraid we are worshiping freely far too many things. With our Creator being a jealous God, I am sure it would be spiritually profitable for every one of us to be very careful and more observant. At least God tells us very plainly to do such. The love of money is the root on which all evil grows, God does not need it.

Of course, Mystery Babylon is only found in the *Bible* one time so, very few people know about it. Very few read the Bible anymore. The Rome Beast has gone into perdition. The beast rider, Mystery Babylon Church, has been sitting on its head ever since. They think they must capture ever country and the world by killing all other people that will not join their church. The Muslims coming up has the same "Join or Die" religion. This is the reason for all our trouble in the end times, one can find all truth in the Bible. Any religion that kills to get converts is not a Christian religion.

Two religions, both with their own *Join-or-Die* beliefs, trying to join btogether constitutes a big problem. Especially if neither one of them know God. This problem will be the core for the world's dilemma from here on out getting worse every day. Until Jesus has to intervene or there would be no flesh left. It will come down to; there will be only three religions in the world. The two named in the previous paragraph, and the Jewish religion which are to except Christ with the Christians.

Better said, the Christians will have to except the Jews, after all Jesus Christ is a Jew and they are God's chosen people. It is only after the first resurrection and God has pulled and resurrected his chosen few out of the world and set them up in a safe place with the Jews in a place called in the Hebrew tongue, Armageddon. Dake may not agree with me but I place *Armageddon* as in the mountains there around Jerusalem. Many a scripture refer to it, but the name is only in the Bible one time.

The twenty-forth chapter of Matthew, verses twenty-nine through the thirty-first verse says it best, then finished and exclaimed it in the seventeenth chapter of Revelations. Our forefathers whipped about all of Europe, with God's help, to obtain the liberty to worship as one pleases. Now we are divided into every belief on the earth without the Bible and giving the Bible away like it is worthless. Looking like Satan won the war after all if he can take our Bible, for that was what it was over, and all we have left. Rome was determined to do away with it. They are still trying to figure out how they failed.

God says Satan will wear the saints out in the last days. In the beginning, God's people seem to me to have started out waring with Satan's people almost constantly. God telling them to kill and annihilate Satan's people completely. With God's people having more compassion on them than their own brethren, and Satan having more patience than any bunch of God's people and does not care who is destroying who. Will bring about the end God described.

Look over a little accurate history and see how long Satan has been dragging this country down daily to the very bottom. The world worships their government as God and wants to kill anybody that refuses to join them. They are the most religionist organization on earth. Joining the Christians and taking them over is how Satan obtained the control of this country and intends to hang onto it the same way.

He learned that from taking England. Our country is so ill taught and so dumbed-down, we do not know the difference between God's people and the Devil Possessed people. Without the Spirit of God, we never will. This fact reinforces my burden to wake a few of God's people up. This world is divided into two kinds of people, God's and Satan's. Where are our preachers that are preaching Truth? Which is Jesus Christ (The Bible: The Word: The Spirit: The Savior: Life itself)? It is hard to discern what our preachers are preaching anymore. Self, I believe.

Our Mystery Babylon Colleges are the ones that trained them, putting them to sleep trying to unite everybody into one belief, atheist. How can a people like that, govern our country, when they cannot govern themselves? Mankind cannot fill a thimble full of people that believes there is no God, the evidence is just too big to deny. Most all the people that say they do not believe in a God are just lying and trying to convince themselves but know better. Satan is the only thing they have left to look to. Therefore, Satan is their god.

The people of the world have been raised, taught, and trained that they are to serve a false god, each man is his own god. That is how many false gods there are. Mystery Babylon Church will except any religion called god, long as they will come under the Pope. Even the Muslims will accept Christ as a good prophet, but not as the Son of God. Most of the U.S. non-believers don't want to go that far.

Without the Son of God, we are carnal, and God will not accept anything carnal. It will never stand in God's presents, it must be a sanctified religion excepted by God first. That requires the Spirit of God, nothing else can save. One does not have to be very intelligent to see that. If he will look and quit believing lies as God has told us to do.

Man's Government just does not look like a God to me, certainly not a God I would trust my soul, family, and country to. They look, and act to me like a *Dragon* without legs. Which I believe was the serpent in Adam and Eve's time, before God put him on his belly. Have you ever seen a dragon?

Who can tell us what a dragon looks like?

I have seen a lot of serpents crawling on their bellies, some of them tens of feet long. How long is a Dragon? God has had to make a lot of changes in our creation to keep man alive. And to keep a few he can save. But God will never change his Word. It is a shame, but God's people do not seem to grow or increase without *persecution*. Guess what, God will have some increase in these last days. God will let Satan drive to him the ones God saves. Jesus will be helping him a little there in end times. The people will become harder to drive in the last days.

Seems we never learn anything, while we think we are learning everything. God says, thinking we are becoming wise, we have become fools. There is a lot wrong with man's thinking in his mind, or spirit.

Without the Spirit of God being the life in him, he is dead, God says do not grieve his Spirit. God has given us a lot of leeway, but God's Spirit will go back to God in due time either with or without us. The ones that do not have it will go to hell and to dust, for eternity.

The world, especially America, seems to operate on the theory that the most influencing thing on this earth is sex. They can hardly advertise anything without hanging a picture of a practically necked person beside it. I reckon that is to get attention, and it does. If they would read their Bible, they could see that it also gets God's attention. Sex has been the major ruination of God's people from the beginning. Just shake a little "Sex" in front of most people and they go completely Coo-Coo.

Adam and Eve was ashamed when they were caught necked. The first thing God did was made them some cloths. Man has been trying to do away with shame ever since. Most of our movies and TVs today are not fit for a grown person to watch but shame is hard to see anywhere, anymore. We think our movies are a sexually stimulating, entertaining, masterpiece. I guess at least part of that is true, but a Christian is expected to know better if he has been taught anything.

The only reason God made male and female with different origins, was for reproduction purposes. He commanded them to multiply and fill the earth. We have let that get so out of control we are aborting and killing or increase to the tune of multi-millions to control our overcrowding. Nobody wants to be responsible for raising them but seem to enjoy having them.

People are lacking for love for anybody but themselves, especially for God. We have about filled the earth but have not produced enough righteous people to fill God's table. We are aborting and killing more people than we are producing or saving. God is going to establish himself a full table even if he must kill off the earth and start all over *again*. He already did that once.

In every case where it seemed sex got out of control by not receiving proper control and respect. God has sent upon the world a very bad contagious terminal disease directly related to sex. God has showed in every word and act in the Bible that he has no favor toward adultery, fornication, sex or a need for it. I have never read it being mentioned in the next world, but I have heard it preached there. It is one of the biggest side tracks in our world, and like a handle on a frying pan for Satan to use on all individuals; to defeat God's plan. We are cautioned to be careful.

When Adam and eve failed God, they died. God turned from mankind and had nothing to do with them until man started calling on God. He turned back to them and started a plan to redeem them that would call on him and love, fear, and obey him. Them that would not, would die as beast, being the vast majority of them. I do not see where he counted Adam and Eve as one of them that repented. Man was not pleasingly acknowledging God, mostly not giving him the love and attention, they needed to, and would not hear, fear or obey him. That meant they did not know him.

If they did not know him meant they had no hope. Knowing God is man's only hope. God holds all the future in his hand, man must call out to God to have any part in it. Study the Bible, the only way is made plain in the Bible. It says to seek God with all one's heart.

CHAPTER 3

GOD'S PEOPLE ARE DIFFERENT

God chose to separate himself out a people, the ones that would call on him to be his people and he would bless them abundantly and allow them to set an example for all the others, that they might call on him. Among the first things he commanded them was to separate themselves from the Devil's people. Them that did not want to cooperate would be sent back into the world away from God's people and die there with their own choice. Very few people have fully excepted that plan from God.

He has not clearly reviled just how he will separate them, but plainly has only excepted a very few. Saying mankind means nothing to him. He has them by the billions but has only chosen a small handful of them.

Abraham had become a friend to God, he told him to take his people and get out from the rest of the people, and he would give him plenty choice land to raise his people on forever. They were to raise their people unto God. God would see after him and his, with a close relationship between themselves. Abraham had the freedom to take in whosoever he pleased, him and his dependence were to depend upon God to be with them as long as they would stay in touch with, fear, and obey, God. Abraham was to be the spiritual father to God's people forever.

The very fact that God provided for and increased his people, and told them to take Satan's people's land, even to kill them off of it. Tells me loud and clear he intended to bless this earth with a God-loving and God-fearing people. But just could not convince the people to love and believe him. They hated righteousness instead. God knows such people would never be happy with him in eternity. Why he has chosen so few to be with him, God does not desire unhappy people to be with him. They will be tried, tested and proven or God will not take them. Many people will be disappointed when God choses his people from among us.

God said the inhabitants of the earth are nothing to him, they are dead unless they are born-again. How could he make it any plainer? God is not going to change heaven to please man. Man is just overbearing and selfish enough to think he should; but that is the reason there will be so few to make it there. I picture the reason God was so happy building this creation, he did not have any people there to tell him how to do everything.

If I had to guess, I believe Abraham being a human and much like us today; too many times he probably waited until he was in trouble before he talked to and called upon God. God did not complain about having to pick him up once in a while but the people he was raising, too many were going astray.

God has said he desires a close relationship with his people and is always ready to hear us and told us how he is to be approached. While we insist on doing things our own way. Man's way has never worked and never will. What man do you know that you would like him to be the direct and constant ruler over you down to the smallest details? Do I hear an answer?

Most men fill the same way and just do not have an answer unless he gets it from God's Word. Don't let man tell you he does if he cannot verify it from the Bible.

Only after Christ came and died for man, did man receive a mediator between each man and God. There was no man living that was acceptable to do the job. God sent the best part of himself to be exposed to all mankind, hoping man would approve of and accept him. When Jesus came back to the disciples among the first few things he said to them was, *"I have been given all power on heaven and earth."* It was plain God excepted Jesus over any and all of mankind. I do not believe we aught to complain about Christ. He is one's only hope.

In the Bible story where the Sons of God saw the women were fair to look upon, took them as wives and renowned men, giants, and evil, was born upon the earth. I cannot confirm just the reason they chose the women, but I can tell what happened. Another plan of Lucifer's to mix, cross bred, and confuse God's people and destroy God's plan for a righteous bunch of people to occupy the earth.

They produced great renowned men and giants on the earth. Evil took it over. God spent some time in killing and breeding the giants completely out of the human race. David and his men killed one of the last few of them, but some survived after David. They must have been from David's wives. God said David's men killed them. The Bible says the named-giant had four brothers, when David went to meet him he took five perfect stones with him. It might have been just a coincidence, but there are very few coincidences in the Bible. Every word of it has a purpose and will be full-filled before the end of time, I believe David was ready for all of them giants. He only needed one for each giant.

David, in going after this giant, asks who is this man that has the army of God scared to a halt and at a stand-still. I believe he was a little perturbed, and in disbelief of what he saw. He thought he could do something about it and did. God favors that kind of man. David had become very accurate with his sling, practicing hard while he was guarding his father's sheep. A giant is no match for a ruddy red headed kid with God in him. We need some David's today to kill a few giants and get God's people started moving again.

One probable will not do many great things without working at it and seeking God. David had proven God in everyday life, he knew what God could do, he did not need armory and a shield and was surely smart enough to know he could not whip the giant without God's help. It was all he needed. Ever wonder how David read that commandment: *thou shall not kill?* David knew the rest of God's Word also, which most people of today do not. It is painfully obvious that the majority of our preachers do not either. This being our biggest sore spot.

I believe the word *kill* applied in and among God's children, as all the Bible is written to do. The authority from God for the sentence of death is given to the congregation. It is to decide what is legal, necessary, or not. The laws to the congregation is laid down like on everything else. I have learned not to listen to the Devil's people preaching the Bible to me, even if he calls himself a spirit filled preacher, all spirits are not of God.

God said to establish every word from the mouth of God with at least two or three witnesses from God's Word as to how it is used before you can call it a Gospel Word for preaching. The word kill must have a few dozen ways one can establish it in use. I'm sure today if David killed a few giants he would have an army of giant supporters trying to kill him. The worlds people, working for Satan, love to see God's people get killed or shipwrecked in any way they can. If you don't believe that saying, just look at our President Trump that God put in office. He cannot turn around but what Satan's people are preaching hate and destruction at him.

He has gotten so many enemies trying to kill him with any way possible. I know people that hate him and will tell you they do, and don't know why. Maybe they should look at the spirit that is leading them and seek a man of God that might help them, instead of Satan that they are a slave to and lost control of their own minds. God has said we are slaves to the one we lend the parts of our bodies to.

Speaking of sex, God has outlined all duties and authority for men, women, children and most of their close kin in any household.

It certainly is not fifty-fifty with the man of the house, in anything. Like I heard a man say in preaching on TV just last Sunday. He was supposed to have been preaching from God, but God did not give the man and woman a fifty=fifty in nothing that I ever read.

Show me a place in the Bible where God placed a man and women fifty-fifty. But mankind thinks he knows better than God, without knowing how to read God's Word. There is nothing worth carrying home, if God is not in it. God abides in nothing that is carnal, including mankind. God has never turned anything but carnal over to carnal.

There should not be any big disputes among God's people. But it is about impossible to get along without a Bible between them and somebody that knows how to read and explain a few things from it. The Bible will answer any question if you will study it with the help of the Spirit. The only spiritly written book we are given, and not to be changed, ever; and never will be.

The problem is simple, most people will not except God to be over themselves. Especially the women and the men with feminist character, they will cause a problem every time. Jesus is the Word of God and able to lead every man, pleasing to God the Father. If not they just as well be ready to allow themselves to be covered up for they are dead while they are still walking.

No one must need to like it but needs to be ready to bury people like those that are supporting California, New York, Chicago, and all left headed places like them. If one is not ready to put the dirt on them then he will be buried with them. For God has spoken, they will be buried.

I do not believe one can easily find someone close to my age that *has not* heard the saying; *Truth Hurts!* But one might be pressed to find one among our young people that *has* heard it. I wonder what has happened? They just learn to ignore the truth, and no pain! They think. But no one will escape God's Word, even though he thanks he can. Look at the slow destruction of California and New York and they will take down everybody that tries to help them. To put

Democrats back in power is the only aim any of them have in sight, not caring one thing about any other person or the country or our future. Especially not for pleasing God.

Just about no situation will work out right for a family up to a nation, if the Word of God is not in the lead. You would think any man could look and see _that,_ even if he did not read his Bible. That is just some of the common sense I keep writing about that men have rejected.

God stated; "In end times the women would rise and rule over the men, and the children would be their princes." We see that becoming very active today in our country and should be smart enough to know to rebuke it. It does not make common sense. Women are organizing and marching and protesting for more authority and more free time out of the home, to protest more, I reckon. Women should read their Bible and see where their duty and responsibilities lie, the same with men; God has explained it to them. Does not God have the authority to tell them?

If our nation would get saved, we would not need maybe a third of the people we have in government. I do not believe we need them anyway. Certainly not above God. They just think they need the job and authority that goes with it, so their buddies created it for them. They are busy scratching each other's backs. Money settles everything; who is caring for the people?

God has plainly laid out duties for every person, saying, "If a man could not control his own house, I do not want him trying to control mine." Some of this teaching that we have perverted and left off in our homes are what is wrong with this country today. Actually, we have destroyed the homes.

I cannot explain how a person can be a Christian and not want to read in the Bible with the Spirit of God helping him. It is the way to learn more about God, or anything else. He tells us plain just how a family should be taught and raised. God is still in control, anyone that cannot except that is among the dead and part of the problem because they cannot raise people unto God.

God knows that fewer and fewer people is going to receive him, as the end approaches. Men seem to only have time to help themselves and tear others down. Only the ones that have the Holy Ghost in them will survive and they will have to be with Christ and the Jews at Armageddon at the end, the rest will take the Mark of the Beast or be killed, or both. This is speaking about the natural man that does not know God.

The Mark of the Beast being an oath against God and accepting a computer-run brain. Read your Bible close if you want to see it. I have written about it in every book I have wrote. Any man that thinks he looks taller by the men he has cut down around him is not a man that will fit in the kingdom of God. He is to be pitied but not promoted.

I wish to slide in a few facts in about here. The Spirit of God is the life of anything that has any life in it. We should be able to look at the animals and creatures and see a little of the verity of life God can install in anything.

Without the Spirit of God given unto a man he is just another animal with a little more talent than most. If he has excepted the hand and call of God he has become born again. A new and completely different Spirit operating his person with a different view of everything, and I am sure he will be noticeable unto anybody that knew him well.

He will likely have to change many of his close friends, not out of necessity just that personalities will be changed and will not fit the same anymore. Of course, most true close friends will understand and adjust to the change, but many will work hard, sometimes to a harmful degree, to try to get back the old person they are about to lose. It is just that a person should be warned, Satan will use every person he can to try to shipwreck any soul he is about to lose.

I am a little like a bulldog about my King James Bible being the only map and guide man has. In around sixteen-hundred AD England was being led off by the Mystery Babylon Church there at Rome which is talked much about in the new testament. They were being led off in so many different doctoring and being divided and confused until they were sounding like America today. Anybody should know there is so many confused churches in America today that all of them cannot be pleasing to God, more like none of them are. Anybody should know this is not of God and is taking America down as God said it would.

The King James Authorized Translation is the only book that can qualify sufficiently to lead us together into one. It is common sense. England sought God for a book that would bring them together in unity and would be blessed by and pleasing to God. Jesus moved on the King of England to authorize and oversee the making of it, after Tyndale's dying prayer, while being burned at the steak by Mystery Babylon headed there at Rome.

James called together a great committee, I believe fifty at the start, of the best English Scholars they could find to screen the scriptures of the world to put together the Book. They would all have to agree on every book and page that it was the very best they could do, and no man was to be left out. And no man's feelings or beliefs were to be let guide any word in it. They did not use a man's quote in it that was not mentioned by Jesus or one of his disciples. Putting the Bible dating back behind Jesus.

They worked on it for at least seven years, purchasing everything that was considered scripture, for screening. Came up with what Jesus said; _"He wrote and did not want a word in it changed nor diminished from, nor added to."_ Even said it was him in person. It was the Spirit of God, it was the light, the way, the life in anything that had life in it; it was _everything_. He wrote it in the _English Language_ and made it into the leading language of the world until today and the only language in the world wrote by Jesus.

Every word in the King James, none more.

Jesus told us to preach it to the world, and to the Greek and Hebrew and every creature in the earth. English is definitely the God given language for God's people. Not the whole English Language, just the words used in the Kings James Bible that Jesus said he wrote.

Every other word on earth is a carnal word English or not. That is not to say that some of them are not good and helpful, just that *man* can stretch the meanings of them to his lacking and there is not scripture to correct him, in his eyes.

Words in the King James Bible are to be established by the Bible. Man thinks he is the truth, but Jesus is the only one that can fill that seat. The Bible is Jesus Christ without any word in it being changed in over a thousand years. Since the testators have died.

One can find people any day that will use any sort of a Bible with any of his personal interpretations trying to explain and correct the King James Bible. There is no such language or books on the earth. Jesus used anything he needed out of the old Bibles and what he did not use he did not need and what he did not need he did not use.

The King James is him as he has said it is, and he did not want nothing changed, diminished or added to any one word in it, said if one could not believe every word, one did not know God. Not one word in the Bible has been changed in over a thousand years. Can we not read what he said? Some people just enjoy calling him a liar. They are guaranteed to fail and perish; with hell waiting for them.

I see the Bible as making the English Language into two languages. The words Jesus used in the Bible, I call the Spiritual Language. The remaining words of the world are a carnal language, English or not. With Jesus saying he did not want a one of them entered into his book that he wrote. He did not want ought to be diminished from a word in it and it could never be changed. It was everything about life any man needed. I wrote in some of my other books, it was the Language that God took away from the earth at the tower of Babel, or at least equal to it.

Not one word has been altered in it in over a thousand years. Show me another book that one can say that about. I know one can find any day all kinds of people that will tell you that is not so; but ask one of them to show you where Jesus lied to us. I will believe Jesus over the world any day.

God commanded his people to put the heathens out from among them. They do not know how to speak our language or how to read God's Word. A new convert needs to be taught how to read the new Spiritual Language. It will be impossible for us to do that if we cannot read, teach, and understand it ourselves. Probably is impossible for us to do now anyway, with most of our people preaching, …..*no borders for this country and no control over its increase in Godless people from all over the world. Giving them more freedom and power than any of God's citizens have; and telling us that is how our constitution and Bible reads;* "*liars."*

With such lies as; *our freedom of worship only applies to false gods. Muslim speaking people know God better than we do, so they have all the privileges from our government and country, many such lying things.* But God's people are told to separate themselves from them, don't let them come into your house. You can see why Obama hated the Bible so much and outlawed it from everywhere he could. Including taking it from the hands of a Navy Champlin, jailed every Christian he could. The very believing-people condemns him to hell without saying a word. We do not have very many of them kind in this country any more.

Nothing different from the King James Bible will ever please God. Like I already wrote, I do not need Satan's people preaching it to me. Yet now, I am allowed to keep them out of my house according to the commands of God. Anyone trying to bring in another religion than *Christ and he crucified*, God said to not receive them into one's house.

God has never advocated for a man to give up authority in his own house nor accept government, which has no authority into spiritual affairs, as one's higher authority over God. God's people should brace to protect the few rights we still have, save our country and us while we still can. We only can if we work together as one. You say that God's people would get too over-bearing If we had all that freedom. God allows our laws freedom to correct us if we get out of God's control.

That is just how far we have gotten away from God. Of all the churches and preachers, I have never heard *that* preached or taught. It would not be safe to preach it, anywhere in public in our country, today. Thanks to our spineless preachers and politicians of the past and present, this is not a Christian nation any more. One is not allowed to live like one; anymore.

Obama said so and I did not hear a soul disagree with him but a country that voted him in as president twice. I wonder how the pilgrims, up to our forefathers, would have reacted to somebody teaching *their* children they could not worship Jesus and God the creator of this world in this country?

The Clintons and Obamas (Democrats) have gotten this country down so low I seriously doubt if we ever see Spiritual daylight again. If we do not repent and take some serious action to remove many of them Obama holdovers and career sold-out Republicans that cannot get their eyes off them billions of dollars floating around Washington. We may never get our heads above the sludge of the swamp again. Over twenty-three-trillion dollars under, a figure hardly heard of before Clintons and Obamas came around and sold about everything they could get a penny out of. If we put all them lying thieves in jail we would have all our prisons over filled. If we could find enough rope, I would consider hanging them. If you are one of them kind of people, you can see right here what I think of you.

There is a lot of people thinking they have the power of God all over them, but have they been tested? God has said, he will have a tried, tested and proven people. We are told to judge ourselves. I am told to judge no other man but to preach God's word to the world, they will have to do the judging. But how can a professing Christian vote for a Muslim President twice, and say he reads his Bible? Some people have no problem with lying. If they did they would choke to death on the lies that fill the air in and around this country today.

We are told our mind is to let the light of the gospel shine into the heart, so one might be saved, and we can have the mind of Christ. If one cannot control his own thinking, he is consistently in grave danger. Someone that will kill many innocent people for no reason, cannot control his own thinking, so he is out of his mind. The same for anyone that will condone or protect such a person, lawyers included. They have had no godly teaching or have let dope, money, and Satan take control of his mind, and that means he is out of control. God calls that Devil possessed. Our country is becoming Devil possessed, if it is not already there.

We have taught *out* all common sense in our schools and homes today. The Bible is forbidden by our Mystery Babylon Government to be mentioned in our schools. Common Sense is what God is all about and we are not allowed to teach such a thing. We are commanded to let the government do our thinking for us. Show that to me in our Constitution or Bible and I will eat it. The bill of rights are for individual freedom, not for government freedom. The more one is educated in our schools today, the farther from God he gets, if he does not have someone teaching truth to him, he is mindless and lost.

They are crying *"What is wrong with our country and our kids?"* It is no wonder why God says we are blind and deaf. It is because we are *blind and deaf* and have given all control to the Mystery Babylon Church there at Rome. Or maybe Springfield, Missouri. The school teachers and politicians have been brain washed and are teaching it to our children is the root of our problem. They told us they were going to do just that. Our country was just so greedy and could just see so much money and power floating around for the taking was just too tempting. Anybody that would not pick it up was just a fool was their thinking.

There is not a more dangerous person on the earth than an educated greedy fool with no common sense. Turned loose, he is a killer. A little more common-sense thinking is needed around the house. Scientist think considering different sexes is a waste of precious time to their fast way of thinking and living and progress. God has never bound them together other than marriage and we are taught that in old fashion.

Different sexes think differently, a child thinks like a child, a woman thinks like a woman, a man should think like a man, one that is God's man *will*. Don't even think that there isn't a difference. We need to learn that from the Bible, our schools are not teaching it, our country does not know it. Our parents and homes do not give a darn about it. God has told each of us how to think and what to think on. Everything he has said is for our benefit. If it doesn't come from off the Bible, take it with a spoon of salt.

Even when he pours out the Wrath of God on the world, it is on people that have taken the Mark of the Beast, to pled with them to repent and for a five-month period they cannot die but will be living with and on, a man-controlled life-giving machine. I am going to think that is the life of them. Jesus is the one that is doing the torturing trying to get them to repent before they die. Even though they blame everything on God. They are correct in thinking he is the one in this case.

The war that about annihilated the tribe of Benjamin until the remaining tribes had to give it people to replenish that part of Abraham's race of people, was fought over perverted sex. The burning of Sodom and Gomorra that appears to have been something more than a nuclear blast that blew the ground down eight feet below sea level in at least one spot. That was once some of the most fertile and watered ground on the earth. Leaving only Lot and his two daughters to replenish that quarter of Abraham's race of people. Sampson's demise was brought on by his lust for sex.

These were God's doings because of perverted sex acts and fornication. I could go on and on with facts about such things, but I believe you can get my drift. Sex is a powerful mover when it comes to mankind. It has been known to change the world. Where do you reckon the words sodomy and gonorrhea deases came from? Reckon Sodom and Gomorra had anything to do with them? We are teaching our children there is nothing wrong with such things, but God says different.

God has worked hard, within the limits of his words and prophecies, to wake people up to the reality of consequences. All overboard sexual action has consequences usually not pleasant at all.

Mankind hates to admit that God is overseeing every movement on this Earth. They seem to believe he is just over the bad things that are happening, they take credit for the good. How stupid?

He gives us everything according to what we ask for, need, want, and *deserve*. Only them that know and trust God, can receive that statement. Only them that believe God can know God.

He is always right, whether we know it or not. The none believer will be held accountable if he has been told. God has told every one of us to preach God's Word to ever creature on the earth. What did that leave out?

It is always a losing proposition to go against God in any way. Some things may look profitable on the short run, but it will show up in the long run every time. If we will just keep score we will soon see the only lasting thing is Truth.

Man has never learned to run things on his own. There must be a few thousand reasons. The first is there is always a few thousand people that can and will get involved and probably cannot get two of them to completely agree on anything. It is hard to get two people to see anything alike. That is not getting a problem started, it is just one that exist and always shows up. The reason all things will only work when it is done God's way. He brings all things into one. Hard for man to fully understand.

This is hard for man to except. Only when one is fully alone and does not involve any one else can he be turned completely lose to do just as he pleases. God is the only thing that can be fully trusted to do things to the best possible way for all things.

CHAPTER 4

GOD'S JUDGEMENTS CAN GET RUFF AND PERMANENT

I had one of them Mystery Babylon members explain to me the reason they could not let the people read the Bible for themselves. She said they would not interpret it alike and would be nothing but confusing to all the people. So, she was a safe Mystery Babylon member. I guess Jesus was a fool for turning such a confusing book loose to the people. He should have just designated from the beginning Mystery Babylon to run his church and sent all the remaining churches to hell. I reckon that is what they think he has done. Her church should read, God said everybody should establish every word that comes out of the mouth of God with at least two or three witness from God's Word.

Did the Mystery Babylon Church die for any of you? How come they refuse to believe in his Spirit and teach the Pope as God and savior to their Church when the Pope has never stood in the gap for any of them and demands them to pay money to him for anything he does? Can you picture Jesus doing that? How do they preach a resurrection? Is their church going to resurrect all its members and present them to God who is a Spirit when they do not believe in a

Spirit? I cannot answer one question, and never heard them answer a one.

They teach their people to not discuss such things with such people as myself. Afraid I might convert one of their paying customers, I guess. A good church that preaches Jesus Christ needs some of your money, but the people will do all right.

The Word of God must be taught and verified from the Word of God. The Word of God tells us just how to do that, but I don't know very many men that seems to know that. Even fewer that are seen practicing it.

When God sent the flood in Noah's time, probably the worst catastrophe on record (not on our record, we are not allowed to put it in our records).

Mystery Babylon does not believe there was ever such a flood even with evidence on every continent.

Some of the Left-headed, God-hating, politicians, and school teacher's children might see it and start asking questions. You know they cannot handle that! So, we are not allowed to teach from the Word of God in a Mystery Babylon school house. God gave us a complete record of the whole thing, in the sixth chapter of Genesis, and why he did it. If one wants to know anything about history, read your Bible. One will not learn it in our government-controlled schools. It would cause confusion in the lied-to children of Christian's. One cannot prove or back up lies, they will just not hold water.

Sons of God saw the daughters of men, thought they were fair to look upon, took them for wives, giants and mighty evil men were being born upon the earth. Violence had filled the earth. God was very hurt and disappointed, they had wrecked his plan with sin and adultery. God decided to destroy the whole thing, but Noah found grace in the sight of the Lord, he had been living upright and fearing God. God had Noah to build an Ark then he washed away every air breathing creature on the earth, except Noah and his wife his three sons and their wives, with enough animals on the Ark to replenish the earth. Another time sex and reproduction had perverted the whole earth.

They teach in our country there was no such thing as a flood like God described in his Word, when there is evidence of it on every continent in the world. Mystery Babylon from Rome does not want it taught, so we will not teach it. I have read in several books, maybe seventy years ago, that every isolated tribe of people found on the earth were carrying, through the ages, some sort of a story of God getting angry and sending a flood upon the earth that destroyed the whole earth and allowed it to be replenished again. I have heard very little about that in several years.

I believe Satan has succeeded in about teaching it out of most of humanity as not being true. There is a lot of things that will disappear if Satan can just get rid of the Bible. You can see his effort trying to do that in any direction you look. Who would you think would want to outlaw and get rid of the Bible, which is Jesus Christ himself? Do you think them are God's people? The Pope has started an effort, along with the Democrat Party and Liberal Left, to do just that.

God said, if you cannot believe the record he gave us of his son, you are none of his. There are a lot of people today claiming to be his that are none of his. Over and over, God has commanded his people, one must believe his Word, or they are *out*. The Word has been the King James Bible since around sixteen-hundred AD. It is the one Jesus claims to be him and he wrote it, period. I do not know of any other book he claims in any such way. He does not need another. He denounced ever other book that does not agree with it.

I do not know of one Denomination that can truly say they believe all the Bible. They lay it to different interpretations, but where do they get the right to interpret the Bible their way? God says the Word of God is to interpret every word of itself with at least two and three witnesses from other places in the Bible as to the way it is used, that would solve the problem. God has never asked man to interpret his word, What denomination did God say would interpret his word?

People that do not want to believe the Bible, God said he would send them strong delusions to believe a lie so that they all might be dammed. Explain that one to yourself; Romans: one.

Mystery Babylon organizations have just about sunk this country, and Antichrist will finish the job. When will the God-fearing Christians ever wake up? Look in your Bible and count the times God's word has ask his people to wake up, seems no one can hear him. We had rather hear a Liberal Antichrist Democrat preaching and lying, anytime. He promises us all kinds of good things from his god the government with our money.

Who will tell me they would not trade everything they have attained to keep from spending an eternity in hell if they believed God or could see it.

If we resented being called asleep we would be reading and teaching the Word of God to our children and one another. The Lord is coming back for his when the ones that are asleep starts running things, and only them that are resisting them will be taken. A fact that I have been wanting to say about what is wrong with this country. God has told us to *train* our children up in the fear and admonition of the Lord and when they are old they will not turn from it. A glorious promise we should cherish.

This studied deep and practiced will solve our lost and out of control crimes, that I have been referring to. Nothing else will work for we cannot do one thing about them without the help of the Lord and starting young. The only way I see to get the help of the Lord is to study the Word and do what it says. If you refuse to do that, you might as well go pray to a black-gum stump. You might draw a crowd, make some money, but move awfully few stones for God's people.

Someone said the other day, that Jesus might come any day, I said, no, he will not come until he can hear his people crying out for him. I will assure you it will get bad enough they will be begging him to come if we keep going the way we are going, and we will. We have allowed this to come upon us, he always answers when his people cries out to him sincerely. You can bet they will. Right now, there are more of them crying out against him. They will be shaken off in the great end-time shaking God's Word mentions, many of them are just barely hanging on now, and producing no fruit for the kingdom of the Lord.

God has said he will have a tried and proven people, he will do what he says. If you feel condemnation, it is not coming from God, it is from the Devil, that is his job, you do not need to listen to him. A sure way to get a front seat in hell. He will have you running and worrying oneself to death, God has said just repent and try to do better. Repentance includes being sorry for, listening and turning to God.

Study God's Word, it is our only road map. We must let it guide us all the way. Far too many people have drawn their own map, this is very dangerous for anybody, or anyone that will listen to them. I have never seen a college professor's map that I considered to be worth a dime toward pleasing God. The King James Bible is the only book on earth, written with a spiritual pencil. Jesus is the Spirit.

Satan has been building up a force against Jesus Christ since the time of Jesus' birth, it has been growing ever since. God calls it Mystery Babylon; its headquarters is at Rome, Italy. It ends up merging with the Antichrist's ten kings coming from the East with its ten horns. (Ten kings that have no kingdom as yet). Ten horns are ten kings and will consist of, at the end, every soul whose name is not wrote down in the Lambs Book of Life. Before it is thrown by Jesus Christ with the Devil himself into the Lake of Fire that burns forever after the battle of Armageddon where the Antichrist and False Prophet will already be.

All judgments will be over, and the New Heaven and Earth will be seen coming down from heaven with God himself setting in the middle of them. Never are we told we will be taken up to heaven to meet him. Heaven is just space above the earth. There will be many wars and sufferings in the middle of all them happenings, and many deaths.

As I have tried to point out in all my books, the world has many problems and misfit situations. Not one answer can give everybody a profit-plus solution unless everybody can come into a "*one*" in all situations. There is only one that can qualify to be that one, that is the Lord Jesus Christ, and there is only one of him. You cannot come into him and bring yourself with you. You will never fit as one with no other being but Christ and the ones that have become one with him. As the Father, Son, and Holy Ghost are one, so will all God's children be one with them.

The world does not understand Spiritual Math, we will just have to accept his Word. Who else is there to accept, but him? He is the only eternal thing one can point toward, why take such a chance. Man is completely helpless without him.

The next time you help to put a dead friend away, look around where he lived and see what you can miss that he took with him. Anything you can put in his coffin will lay there until it goes back to the earth. Want to try and prove it?

There is evidence somebody has moved stones around on the earth, but it is rare to see evidence where any man ever stood in any place of old, and it is rare to see any man over a hundred years old. How many men do you reckon has come and gone upon the earth? Can you talk to one? I know spirits can put real sounding thoughts in your head. Can you show us one?

You people that think I am sounding crazy, I wonder what a Spirit would think of you and many of your thoughts? Everything you know, a spirit had to give it to you. God says he is not the one who is blind, dumb, and dead, that is a satanic spirit. So, it must be what most people are listening to. Maybe we should get to know our maker, he has both arms open and has told us all things. His Word has the answer to everything. We must believe and trust him, or leave this life not knowing anything.

The smarter we are in the carnal, the more foolish we are in God's eyes. The Spirit sees things from the opposite side than the carnal. The Spirit is correct every time and is going to start over again with only a few of mankind in the new heaven and earth. It is a once in a lifetime opportunity, but God reasons that if you despise him here, you will despise him on the other side. He will not force himself upon anybody. I would rather despise a little here than suffer eternity in hell with no body for my soul. You cannot show me anywhere in the Bible where Satan is going to supply you with a body to get you around. I do not believe he can.

I do not know just how a spirit gets around, but we are told it will not get out of the fire of hell that burns forever and ever. None believers will be in the hell that was prepared for the Devil and his angels. The atheist, Saul Alinsky, Hillary's mentor, said he could hardly wait to get to hell to start organizing a rebellion against God. I believe he thinks he will go there and pick up his new body, how sad. He can see further than I can, I cannot envision that well at all. I fully believe, him and Hillary both will get a chance to see what they can do there. God says all secrets will be reviled. It will be a little late to make any changes.

I talk a lot about Mystery Babylon in all my books, it grew off the beast Babylon and will grow into the largest number of names of souls that anyone has read of on this earth. Consisting of every soul whose name is not listed in the Lambs Book of Life will be in it. (All ruling kingdoms since Babylon is referred to by God as, in a sense, a continuation of Babylon.) I believe God just referred to the number in them as the sands upon the seashores. Can you imagine what the devil can do with that many souls? Except hell will be hotter for him than for anyone there and I do not believe he will be able to get out either.

With friends like Hillary and Alinsky, I do not see how he will be happy there. They do not seem to me like very good friends. Can you imagine just a few of the others that will be there? Like I said in another place, I do not see where they will have a body to be friendly to or with.

Wonder what they will look like, without a body? I hope I never have to see. I believe if we can believe God's Word here, we will never have to see.

The Bible is all about God and our planning to meet him. I believe one can say that is what this world is about, preparing to meet God, not making a spot for ourselves on this earth. We should be preparing for the hereafter. Only God will be there to run it, if you cannot get along with him here you will not be there.

God has promised to take care of us if we will just believe and prepare for him. Look around yourself, what have you got that you could have gotten without him? You could not breathe without him. I will agree with Abe Lincoln, they say he said, "He could not see how a man could be born, look around, and deny there is a God."

There seems to not be a saying, or a deed one can come up with, that some person will not try to do or out-do. God says that man is not only going to destroy himself but destroy every man God has made if he is left unchecked, and man thinks he is so smart. God has made a way for us to be saved, so simple most of us will not receive it. If one is believing and trusting God he is perfect, God has not said one must live perfect, just repent often as necessary. Ever hear it said, one will reap what one sows?

Just look around us and see what is happening with us, and how helpless we are, and that God is our only hope. One cannot do that without denying the flesh of mankind and quit listening to it and turn to God that created us and put our trust in him. He is our provider and protector. Flesh is dead and don't know it. In time it will go back to the dust from which it came, and to the God it chose down here. How many have you seen that has beat the deal God has offered us? There is no escaping it. He is looking for them that will volunteer to completely be in his service and love him for it.

This last few paragraphs have said a big mouthful and is worthy of reading them over again.

God's way is straight and narrow, one can get off on the right or left. God himself is the only close thing on it and is not very tenant to the things of Satan. Which are all carnal. Satan's ways are all full of lies and deceit sounding full of excitement, everything for the flesh, false, and misleading. All Satan's apples are full of worms. Anything he has touched is defiled and needs to be tossed behind oneself.

Any road sign that does not agree with the Word of God should be ignored. Men cannot manufactory one's own road signs and guide anyone to heaven. How hard, fast, and beautiful he can preach should never lead one away from truth, we are each responsible to judge and be accountable for oneself. It will never be any different than that.

If one will not read his Bible and believe it, he will not know much of what I am talking about. I can read, teach, and preach the Bible but cannot have much effect on one's hearing and receiving of it. One must oversee that. I have written much in all my books about how a man should be in control of all his thinking in his heart. For he will be held accountable for all of it. God says, as a man thinketh in his heart, so is he.

With the 2018 elections coming up, I have been sounding off at anybody that will hear. We should send every career politician home that we possibly can. After being elected they all are under attack and tempted to go after the money and power, which equal about the same thing, and plenty of them available through the old hands that has been there a while. I have told my whole family, if I find that any one of them voted for a Democrat I will disown them. (A very small smiley-face goes here.) I believe our old politicians carry around their private milking machine in their knapsack. Some of them should be getting about wore out. Just, get a new one and charge it to the government, I reckon.

I have had Christians shun me and complain about my preaching about politicians, one older preacher told me, the "Bible says I am not to mention the word politics from the pulpit." I searched diligently and did not find the word politics in the entire Bible, reckon it is too dirty for God to use? It is for sure a carnal word. I found the word *pulpit* one time in the Bible where Ezra stood on one to preach the Word to God's people.

I concluded that God had said very little about pulpits or politics, so much for that man's preaching. Most preachers scoff at what God has said and go around preaching what somebody else has told them, *poor* preaching. They are not heard to spot if one is read up on God's Word.

I have become very hardened on the fact that a person should check out things before he repeats them as Gospel. I believe that is a good habit for anyone to grow into and will usually keep your slack-time occupied for a good cause. I have heard it said that bad habits will fall on one, but good habits one must work at them.

You will probably be amazed at the knowledge one can acquire in a short amount of time, with his mouth closed, eyes and ears open. God says, "A man that labors in the Word is worthy of double honor." There is a big difference in just reading and laboring in the Bible for truth. One will not attain much any other way.

The God that created mankind knew what he was doing. He does not look very favorable on man since the first ones failed miserably. God seems a little harder to convince. Jesus loves man so much that he volunteered to pay the price for all of them for the few he could convert that would love him back with a favorable love. I've never read where he called any judges here on earth, any farther than every man is to judge himself, and speak truth.

God warned him that it would be very few that he could save. The carnal people were deaf, blind, dead, and was sold out to the major enemy of God, *Satan*. The back and bottom side of God himself, he had rebelled against God and he must be destroyed, him and all his people. They are liars, selfish, greedy, two faced, self-centered, worthless and could never be allowed to stand in God's glory (sounds like I was describing politicians). They would be consumed instantly in God's presents. Jesus volunteered to be the mediator between God and man for the few he could persuade to be born into his Spirit and live there.

The only foundation we must build on is Jesus Christ, when he comes back and kills Mystery Babylon the Great, Mother of Harlots and Abominations of the Earth, drunken with the blood of the Saints and with the blood of the Martyrs of Jesus Christ and gathers his flock of sheep. It will lead to the end of Jesus' mercy to the world.

He throws Mystery Babylon and every soul whose name is not written down in the Lamb's Book of Life into the fire that burns forever, and ever. Read about it in the nineteenth and twentieth chapters in the book of Revelations, the ending is stated very plain. The next chapter starts in with the new Heaven and Earth coming down to us with God on the throne in the middle of them.

I doubt very much if many of you have heard that side of the Bible preached. Preachers are too busy preaching what people want to hear and what makes them look so talented and smart and will draw a crowd. And will bring in offerings to them, these are the way they measure their sermons. I am persuaded God has no hired hands but pays all his labors.

My preaching does not bring me much praise or glory nor money, that is not what I am preaching for. I challenge any critic to show me where I have gotten out of, or contrary to, the Bible. I will congratulate him and think him kindly and try to correct myself. The only way I will accept correction is with established scripture, the Bible tells us how to establish it. Confirmed or backed up by at least two or three other places in the Bible as to the way each word is used.

That can be reliable only to words found in the Bible. Any other word is carnal and can be backed up to any person's liking. You may not have heard that preached either, I never have. But I have read it in about four places in the Bible. If teachers use it, it would about eliminate all but one confirmed denomination. It would be the established Word of God. Like God said to established it. The Bible is written with Spiritual words and a Spiritual pen. Nothing else is.

Denominations arguing with one another when probably neither one of them are right. They should just get together and establish the scripture, and shake hands, both could go home happy and in agreement. Arguing the Scriptures is a foolish thing to me. I do not know of it settling anything except division and proving that neither one of them do not love truth. Truth is Jesus Christ, God says if you do not love Truth you have no part with him. But as I have already said, carnal despises all truth. And God will have nothing to do with carnal, (Anything apart from the spirit). Without Jesus, no one would be saved. We would all be carnal, or apart from God.

When God wrote, "You will know the Truth, and the Truth will set you free." He was covering a mighty big story, few if any, can understand the gross significance of the small half of that saying. Truth is Jesus, no less. Jesus is the *everything* to mankind. He is the Word of God, every bit of it. The whole of this creation was made through him and some people have the grit to deny him, the Truth.

They not only have forgotten him, they have forgotten the words that refer to Godliness. Like respect, decent, fair, and many more, how do they expect to inherit eternal life? God says to fear him and believe his Word guarantees a place with Christ in the hereafter. I have not read anywhere of a short cut. If one knows Jesus one Knows the truth, if one knows the truth he knows Jesus. You can turn that around all day it will always be true. Truth will always set one free. Lies are spirit-killers, never anything else. Our TV's are filled full of lies even the commercials are sickening to me and to about any sound mind. One can hardly hear one that is not full of lies and one sided to say the least.

Ever take the time to look at the TV and see all the natural, devastating, catastrophes, that have been overrunning the world and our country? Look at a geographical map of our country and see if they do not favor the areas that are most settled in Liberal Democrats and illegal aliens like California, New York, South Eastern Texas, around Chicago, New Orleans. All alone the south and eastern coast. Every once in a while, some midwestern states that are getting a little slack will get a jolt to revive them. They are constantly voting any way that will tear America to the ground, and prophet themselves best.

I have been saying for fifty years now, that I am not at all sure that California will survive until the Lord comes. God has said he will send all these things upon a people that dare forget him, to get their attention. It is for their own good. Check it out, if you don't find it to be so, I will pay for lying. If I cannot show one where every natural catastrophe that is going on in our country today is listed in the Bible and promised to anyone or place that is neglecting God. If that is not true, I will again pay for lying. God says he controls all these things.

It is no wonder God has said we are blind and deaf. He knows the Devil's works and will destroy them all in time. I do not want to be on Satan's side, is exactly why I try to be a good Christian. I got to noticing at an early age, God was having to pull me out of fire, after fire. I decided around the age of thirty-five, maybe I had pushed my luck far enough, and I started trying to pay Christ back for a little of it.

I had somewhat of a reputation across several states, and some in Europe. I could give you a list of crimes that could fill this page that I have been involved in forty years ago, plenty serious. Like counterfeiting, whisky making and hauling, bank robbery. Many more that I am ashamed of. But God has managed to give me a clean record. I have never been sorry for the change I made, not for one minute.

I have always feared and respected God, and that has always pulled me threw. There are people of today that knew me most of my life that have a hard time believing I made such a change. I told everybody since, that there is nothing out there in that world, for if there had been, I would have found it.

I am not trying to boast of myself, I am meaning to boast a bunch about Jesus Christ, he is much to boast about and I would never get tired of it. He is no respecter of person, and full of mercy. I will give you a little clue, when I got on board with Christ I got on with all four feet, just like I've always done everything else, all my life. I have not suffered for that either. I am sure Jesus knew all along what he had in me. I am thankful for that.

Jesus has run my life a lot better than I ever did, and I have had no problem getting along with him. He is still pulling me out of the fire. I was asked a few times what it was that caused me to make such a change. I am sure now, they were expecting a big story. After a short pause, I said, I just got tired of the way I was living, all I could think of at the time.

I tell everybody that one day I will walk into heaven and see a tired, wore out, beat up looking Angel setting over in the corner, someone will be asking him, "What happened to you?" he will answer, "Oh, they assigned me to look after Bill Wilson, his stay down there on Earth!" Thinking that should explain it, I reckon.

God says Angels are encamped around them that fear the Lord. Boy, have I taken advantage of that scripture! He has allowed me to make up for a little of it. I am sure I will never put a ripple in what I owe him, but I try to at least show my appreciation. I believe that is what he appreciates. I read where he said he would have a tried and proven bunch of people. I would not want to leave that scripture out or forget the one that said and wrote it. He is our everything, there will never be a day go by in one's life that we don't need him.

I look up to people that can recognize and appreciate a strait fact, and that is one of them. I sometimes think Jesus is made up of facts, I try to love them even if some of them hurt. They are for the better. *One can do nothing against truth, only for it* and one had better be prepared to meet it.

As far as Jesus is concerned that is what life is all about, though most people think it is about themselves. Just shows how far most people are from God their creator. Our lives are just a chance to be reconciled back to God from whence we all fell. God is long suffering and full of mercy, but stern and dependable. Which most people are not, and fail to understand the quality in things, if they do not know God. They will never understand unless they come to know him, he is our only future during and after this life. We need never forget it.

Spirits have been known to hang around the area where someone lost their life and do wired things for a while known as ghost but are very limited as to what they can do. Ghost is an old English word meaning the same thing as Spirit. I believe that one must believe in them or he will not be apt to hear from one. Is that not true of the Spirit of God? You will not be apt to hear much from him unless you believe in him. Seems to be a characteristic of a Spirit toward mankind.

They different from our spirit and are the superior side of anyone. God has drawn many lines in the sand around us to protect us from bad spirits, or we would not be able to survive. This is also plain in God's Word. If one will study and believe it. God has said, if he needs our attention he will release them spirits enough to get our attention and will help us if we will just call out to him. God is always mindful of us but wants man to learn a few things when and if he takes us in completely. I keep wondering if he will ever get New York, California, Chicago, New Orleans, and some close surrounding areas' attention? I hardly see how they can stay asleep.

God's Word is lined with accounts and stories of humans and spirits having meetings with one another, over and across the line of death. I have been studying and trying to understand more about them, so I might write some on that subject. It is a very deep and complicated subject. Although we know it is not just a thing of one's imagination. The ones that are come and gone can and do act on certain missions with the living.

The witch called up Samuel for Saul, Jesus told of the rich man talking to Abraham. I myself can relate several strange things that I know cannot all be of just someone's imagination. Samuel was not at all very happy for Saul to have called him up. He had already advised Saul on many things that Saul had not listened to him, now why was he bothering him, calling it disquieting him.

It seems that they cannot change things for one once they have passed on but can about tell one all the facts that are straight ahead of them. Maybe they could prepare them selves if they would, but you don't see them getting very excited about it. Like about all living people, its hard to get them to fully receive and believe the truth.

God is the beginning and the end of eternity. Hard for us to comprehend, and only can, as he gives us understanding. All the knowledge man has, stacked up together, is below the foolishness of God. Yet, man thinks he can advise God or hold out on God, but you will not change him. Man, and God lives in two different worlds, Christ, the one that bought and paid the price for us is the sole owner of mankind. He is only going to keep and claim a small portion of all mankind, a proven few. The rest will have chosen the world and will perish with it.

If one doesn't know Jesus, he does not know the giver of life. The Spirits seem to work backwards to the carnal, the more I know, the more I know what I do not know. If that makes any sense to anyone. All that mankind knows, would not make a dent in what God knows.

If it seems to you like I am writing like I am so smart, I want you to know I am just unwinding a little I have read out of God's Word, the Bible. The one Jesus said he wrote. I am a firm believer it covers everything in God's creation. I have hardly scratched the top side of it. I have about used all my seventy-eight years of life reading in it, and fill like I've still got an empty head. If not for the Spiritual knowledge.

The main reason I am writing all these books is to stir up some interest in the Bible. It is for sure God's people are going to need all of it they can get to ride out these last days. We are hardly into them yet, and Satan is attacking them harder every day. God says the Bible is our Light and Life.

We are coming down near the time Jesus said it will be better to die in the Lord than to live from here on out. No need to try blame God, he has told us all things. We can see many of the signs that he said to look for, easily coming upon us. We still have time to prepare, but so few are preparing, it looks shaky for me to look at it. I know I am not going to live long enough to see much of the things that are coming. That might not be a bad thing, but I would like to inform as much of the younger people as I can.

If our country would just let other nations alone and look after our own country and things God has committed to us a little better we could have a much smother road to travel. God has not given the whole world to us to be responsible for. Like Satan tells us all the time and what many of our preachers are preaching. When we cannot teach our own families and or country to be saved, it is for sure we cannot teach other countries how to make it.

People that cannot save themselves are not likely to save very many others. This country was built and blessed to save the world from Mystery Babylon the Great. We defeated her twice in two world wars, but now have let them wear us out like God said we would.

Jesus is going to have to intervene and gather his elect from the four corners of the world to a place in the mountains near Jerusalem called in the Hebrew tongue Armageddon. There are not enough saints to stand up for him against the Antichrist. Told about in Mathew: twenty-four, verse thirty-one. Explained in Rev: sixteenth and seventeenth chapters.

This will be the first resurrection. To save his few Jews and chosen saints to rule with him for the thousand-year reign over the world, to replenish the population of the world to maybe the largest it has ever been. The Devil will be bound and threw into the pit, no tempter left to temp them for the thousand-year reign. Then Jesus will release the Devil that has been in chains of darkness in the pit for a thousand-years. Telling him to go over the world and bring every soul of every country and nation. That is dissatisfied with the perfect rule of Jesus and his first resurrected saints. To war against Christ and his little flock there at Armageddon for the great battle of the Lord God Almighty.

The dissatisfied ones will be the ones that are so carnal they will desire to have charge over themselves and theirs. The Devil will temp and convince them they can easily defeat Christ and his little camp there at Armageddon with the largest army ever assembled on the earth. Anybody that knows anything about Jesus Christ, should know that is not going to be done. But you can see today how many people will take a chance.

Jesus will make a clean sweep of the world and throw Satan and every soul whose name is not written down into the Lambs Book of Life into the lake of fire that burns forever and ever. This is the three beasts that Jesus names. The *False Prophet* and the *Antichrist* that he will throw into hell (The 2 men, for their time is through) and will put a one-thousand-year seal on Satan and put him into the bottomless pit with the one thousand years seal upon him for the millennial reign. Jesus said if he did not intervene there would be no flesh left. He does intervene to save the Jews and his chosen Gentiles this being the first resurrection.

The Gentiles have turned from caring for the Jews and killing them and each other instead, until the world will become nearing the end of all flesh. One needs to believe every word in God's Word for life is in every word. We were created by it and stay alive by it, for as much time as God gives to us. Knowing every one of us will be judged and rewarded by it at the end of the world.

Jesus' intervenes to gather his people, the Jews and his chosen gentiles to a place called Armageddon. Jesus and his chosen saints will be ruling the world from Jerusalem through this one-thousand-year millennial reign; then the Devil will be released, told about in the book of Revelation. All the dead that ever lived, will be called up before the great white throng judgement and him that sets on it, from whose face the heaven and the earth fled away and there was found no place for them.

John saw all the dead, small and great, stand before God; and the books were opened; and another book was opened. Which is the book of life; and the dead were judged according to their works out of those things which were written in the books. And the sea gave up the dead which were in it; and death and hell delivered up the dead which were in them; and they were judged, the total of every man according to his works.

Death and hell were cast into the lake of fire. This is the second death. And whosoever was not found written in the book of life was cast into the lake of fire. Read about it in the twentieth chapter of Revelations. The story is completed there right down to the very end, not that hard to understand.

I have been praying for some time to know what is going to happen to all the kids being born in that thousand-year period called the millennial reign.

Thinking they would be born and dying not seeing the end. Starting in after Mystery Babylon with its False Prophet will be waring with the ten horned Antichrist for some time, the world will basically all be at war.

If one cannot believe the King James Bible is God's Word, like it says it is, you probably will not get much out of it. John saw a new heaven and a new earth, coming down from heaven, for the first heaven and the first earth were passed away; and there was no more sea. No room left for the old creation or the people that did not prepare.

Mystery Babylon's city will be burned from the earth by the Antichrist and killings like mankind has never seen. God has raised the Antichrist up and put it into his heart to kill the hypocrites of Mystery Babylon. But the Antichrist does not know the difference between the hypocrites and true Christians. God will call the Christians out of Mystery Babylon before the Antichrist is turned lose on them. Only the true Christians will hear the Angel he sends to warn them to get out.

For Jesus and his elect at Armageddon this will be heaven for the time. But what about the children being born and dying in that time. This time will bring on a new period of time like we that are living today have not seen. For instance, there will be a new food, and many other things, I have not studied all of it out. Jesus and his chosen resurrected saints will be ruling a perfect rule from his seat there in Jerusalem and the hills thereabout called Armageddon as kings and priest on the Earth.

The first period of time when men started out living to be a thousand years old before God shortened it down for man's sake; is comparable to the thousand-year millennial reign. At the end of time, a long lifespan for mankind is being returned to reestablish and replenish the earth with a population more than it has ever had. With a new food, the Devil locked away, the Antichrist and the False Prophet in hell, and many other changes that Jesus mentioned through the Bible that one can pick up on.

There will be no tempter to hinder and I can assure one there will be no abortions going on in the area Jesus is ruling over things. We cannot compare today's people with people just before and in the millennial reign, there is just too many things different. We only have God's word to study on it.

After the millennial reign, Jesus will release Satan from the pit and sends him forth across the world and nations for his last mission.

Time means nothing to God, but everything to a carnal man. God tells of the day an angel will stand with one foot on water and one foot on sea, and among other things, will announce that time will be no more. It is for sure nothing here will be the same over there.

God told Daniel that the life of England, Russia, and America, will be spared, but says very little about how many people will be spared with them or what shape they will be in. At the White Throne Judgment every soul will be rewarded for the work he has done, good or bad. Every soul whose name is not written down in the Lamb's Book of Life will be cast with Mystery Babylon into the fire that burns and never goes out.

This will be the second death Jesus spoke about. This is above our comprehension, we have only God's Word for it. God's Word is the most assured thing ever, his Word is the only thing that is going to heaven with God at the end unchanged. Where else can you find a book that has been around for one-thousand years and not one word of it has been changed since the testators have died.

It was written by Jesus Christ himself, every word of it, and Jesus said he did not want one word of it moved or changed, not ever. If it has, it cannot be legally labeled the Original King James Authorized Bible, but a modified copy under somebody else's name, then false. God is not obligated to a word in it.

The original is the Lord Jesus Christ himself. It is one sacred and blessed book like no other book ever written. It contains the answer to every problem on this earth. Do you know a man that could write such a book? Jesus was no ordinary man.

He was the Son of God. Finished his assignment as a man and went back into his spiritual habitat. Again, we must rely on the Word of God for the account. And thank England for seeking God for it and proving it for all of us. Historians do not like to tackle the subject. The world is afraid of and hates it. It is loved by them that know God, and hated by them that don't, he is The Spirit.

The Spirit and the carnal are two worlds, the carnal is doomed to pass away completely. God is going to burn up everything of the creation and the heaven nothing will be left but the smoke of the burning. Jesus has said he will make everything new. His people will be setting on the Sea of Glass watching. The Spiritual will be the only thing left. If one does not want to pass away forever he better hang onto the Spirit for it is the only thing that is eternal. Everything about the spiritual side of Satan will be destroyed in a fire God says will never quit burning. Things that are impossible with man are possible with God.

How are we going to argue with God? He laughs at the foolishness of man, if you have a problem, take it to God, it will be taken care of if one can believe. Man has brought every problem he has, upon himself, insisting upon carrying it. God says to lay them all on him, he can carry them, we cannot. We must always be in talking distance with God and able to hear and believe him for safety.

Talking without hearing is a broadcasting station. Hearing without talking is a receiving station, both can equal a conversation. If this country would just close its mouth long enough to look at itself a little, I believe it could see that it is listening to the Devil and not God. God has never told his people they were to take care of the world full of Devil Worshipers, he has said to put them to death.

We refused to obey God when he said for us to separate ourselves from them, and to have nothing to do with them. How can he bless us with us entwined with them and living just like them? God has said he will punish and destroy them and everything that is attached to them. They are plainly the Devil's work, not God's, and he is showing us that every day from every direction. Do we think we are more powerful than God and we are going to save them? God never called us for that, only to preach his Word to them and warn them. He will save them that will become worthy.

God said we were not to have them to come into our house. He said we could help the poor and needy with basic life preserving things any time we wanted to if we had it to spare but did not command us to do that unto the Devil's people. God told his people to come into one and help each other on an equal level, but put the Devil's people out from among you, separate yourselves. When the Devil's people start preaching these things that I have just wrote against, give him some scripture and tell him to leave you alone.

If we do not read our Bible anymore how can we preach to them? I hear people confused and complaining, mad at God and wondering why he does not jump around for them when they are hurt or ask him to. And don't seem to think God is doing what he said he would. I've heard them say they are doing everything they know to do. They don't know much to do.

Have they never read where God has told us to separate ourselves from the sinners and unbelievers? And to put them out from among you? Even if married to them let them be free to go if they would not agree to let you serve God. To not give them God speed, or we are partakers of their sins. We are not to have them into our house. Not to eat with them. No flesh should glory in his presents. We have gotten our country down to Satan's level, and obeying him, we are tying God's hands from blessing us.

I really do not believe that God will send someone to hell for any one of these things I just named but they will discourage and destroy anybody that will let them do it. I could name dozens more, but I was only trying to make a point, God cannot bless one if he has himself tangled with the Devils people, and he does allow us to just get down into the gutter with them until even the crudest sinners can not see any difference in us and them. The Devil demands for us to live down at his level, then he can laugh at us and God, accusing us of being there if we are there or not.

One does not have to be mean to someone to convince them that you are different just witness to them when they require you to help or shire with them. The more you help them, the more you can testify to them.

You will eventually get one saved or drive one away for sure; just obey God in every situation. It will require much prayer and the Spirit of God in any situation.

God has said for his people to stand out, so he can bless you and they can see you are blessed and will be asking how they can get some of that. But if you do not stand out, how can God treat you any different than them or expect any glory from blessing you? People do not think God is worth meditating on day and night, why would he want to follow us around to just get to bless us over and over continually when you don't even have time for him on Sunday morning. Why would we think he is going to have pleasure twenty-fore hours a day in us? Our fellowship is with God and God's people, not with the Devil and his people.

It is not so surprising to see the world's people not being correct at quoting the Bible but seeing so many of our preachers misquoting it and leaving so much of it out is very disheartening. It would be mighty hard for a preacher to spend too much time reading his Bible and seeking God, this will definitely separate one from the world.

Any preacher that is loading God's people up with the cares of this world and looking out for Satan and his people is not preaching for God but is listening to Satan instead. Look at where they have our country at, we are serving the Devil over the world. We do not have no defense if we do not have the Spirit of God in us. If we have it in our minds and heart it will protect us from all Satan's tricks that are blaming God's people for all their troubles. Did you have anything to do with putting them there for Satan to use?!

The Devil has his preachers preaching to us every day, accusing us and loading us down with all the weights of the world blaming God's people for every bad thing, like we are responsible for all the troubles of the world. They do not know how to read the Bible, and when we cannot recognize that, we cannot read it either.

The women that cry how mean and cruel their abusive husband is to them, if you love your husband more than God, what can God or any other people do for you? Cut his legs off? We do have laws you know, try using them.

The Devil has been known to preach the Bible, read what he said to Jesus, and what Jesus said to him. Jesus told Peter once he was preaching the message wrong and was a hindrance to him and called him Satan. One that knows the Bible, knows that Jesus talked to the spirit of a thing, rather than the carnal side. He said if one finds his life here he is dead here with the world and will be burned up with it.

I remember when the people went to church, the church people sat in the front of the church, what we called the Aman-Corner. The none professing people sat in the pews of the house. You could instantly see which ones were professing Christianity and were to be working for the Lord and the ones that were not. That seemed to be the trend all over the country then in Pentecostal churches. Some of them people in the back of the crowd are out-preaching the preachers and teachers, does that sound right to you?

Now there is another side of that fact sometimes the man in the back knows more about the Bible than the one that is doing the teaching, this should not be so. That man should get better prepared in his sermon and stick with it, keep control, or consider letting some one else have the job.

Our weapon is only and always the Word of God, learn to use it. I believe God has asked his people to stand out and be recognized, but you cannot tell them apart today, not even in the church house. I have seen preachers preaching hard in the pulpit and not even have a Bible opened around him. I reckon one is supposed to guess what he is preaching from.

He will be preaching the same things over and over with his church growing very little, if at all. Maybe Christians don't care what they look like to the lost, seems that way in a lot of other areas too.

I guess they could be called undercover Christians, one must ask them if they are saved or not. Who are they working for, Satan, or the Lord, or the people? It is not an easy assignment to preach to the lost. Whether sitting in the front or the back, the word of God is the same. A preacher should learn to preach what God has assigned him to preach, not wait to see what is sitting in front of him. Does one think God does not know who is going to be in church that day, or maybe he knows more about preaching than God?

This country started out for and in Christianity, plainly being called a Christian nation, but we had a Muslim president that took that away from us. The Liberals demanding the religious liberty only applies to a false religion, not to Christianity. I was not surprised that the *world* swallowed their lies and promises, like they were married to a devil and voted him in twice, running our national debt up double what all the other presidents before him together had run it up to.

I guess they were in love with Obama and could not help it, he is a good-looking man. We are told by God himself, Lucifer was a good-looking fellow. It was disappointing to see how many professing Christians voted for him, twice. He told us from the start what he was and what he was going to do and what he was going to do with our money and country.

He was going to distribute it to the Devil's people all over the world and apologize to the world for having a little wealth left as if we are a selfish bunch of devilish people for being blessed by God when we owed over ten- trillion dollars by helping and protecting the world. Over twenty-trillion by the time he left. I think too many people were just as queer loving and Devil possessed as Obama.

Where were God's people at, can they not hear? I'll admit voting was a hard decision to make, but that was our fault. We pushed the ones up there when the Devil himself could see they were God haters. The reason God gave us Obama, we ask for him by our need to see what God haters would do. I have been preaching the left is God haters for over forty years, but I believe Christians should always vote, but vote as godly as one can or how can God use us?

He may not have told *you* he was a Muslim. But he told me what he was from day one. He went around blaspheming God every chance he could get and talking about the Holy Koran and praising Muslims and giving them our money every chance he could find. It appeared to me that our country agreed with ever statement he made. I would be ashamed to call him or them a God-fearing person.

If God did not think we needed him he would not have given him to us. At least he was more honest to us than the ones that run against him. We have some of the biggest liars and hypocrites in politics there are in the world. Obama was not half the hypocrite as some of the others. He said he was a Muslim and what he was going to do with our tax money and our country. Could we not hear and see? Or just did not gave a darn?

I voted and did not vote for Obama but could hardly stomach the one I had to vote for. But none of them stole the money, Bill and Hillary had already done that and gave it all away, what they could not spend or stash in the Clinton charity foundation which was a sickening laugh. If we had a few Republicans with legs and a backbone to hold them up straight, they would be putting them in jail. If it was the other way around they would be in jail.

I did not have enough ground to stand on to argue with them and I still have only the Bible. It is obvious to anybody that knows anything about our history, that God had a big hand in establishing this country. It was not just a miracle that happened along, but we have disowned God and gave this country away. I did decide to start preaching and writing about it. It is time somebody woke up for sure.

I wonder if God would call this a Christian nation, with thieves, queers, liars, and sex perverts running it by vote and our laws, teaching it in our schools as special honorable privileges and demanding our kids love it. And jail time for anybody that says anything different to them. We have plenty freedom for false religions. We make congressman out of them. Trying to jail me for having a gun while they go around with a circle of guns surrounding and protecting them and they are on our payroll.

Most of the politicians are safe, just do not mention Jesus. The kind of people that will shoot them are Devil Possessed too and will rarely shoot anyone but a godly politician. And we have very few of them.

The Devil is teaching us, with success, the Bible is evil and one of the most dangerous books ever printed and is succeeding in having it outlawed in our country. Do you think Jesus would call this a Christian Nation? I don't believe he does. A Christian nation would not stand for such, not to mention supporting it.

God could put the Devil's people out, but he would not have enough people left to run the country or keep it alive, God sure does not have many that is qualified. I can hardly see anybody that can defeat the Devil enough to teach a church. I do not know how long God is going to keep blessing this country. It is starting to look slim and slimmer as the Devil's people are taking complete control of even our churches and ordering Jesus out of them.

The only way I see how God can save this country for the few Christians that are in it, is to destroy the Devil possessed people that are running it now. He is raising up ten Muslims kingdoms in the East for that purpose, they will join the Mystery Babylon Church for to destroy it. God has told us all about it in his Word. But our preachers do not have time to read it. I pray we will repent and not let that happen, but it is looking about hopeless. Can anyone see our Christians protecting this country? When they are throwing them out of our military services.

God says his people are deaf and blind and cannot or will not read his Bible anymore. It will take God's Spirit to put any life back in them and the majority of them does not believe in the Spirit of God, it is easier to do things their way and please the people and get money for it. God will not force himself upon anybody, his servants work for him freely. I do not see them anywhere. Some people will name Jonah to try and call that a lie. Jonah had a choice, he just did not like living in a whale's belly. Show me one place Jonah did not believe God. The reason God spared him.

Jonah had not backslid, if you will read all the story close. He was mad at the people of Nineveh and did not want God to deliver them but knew God would if they would just repent. Jonah said he knew God would. God ask if it did Jonah good to get mad.

People all over are wondering why our country is suffering so much violence and destruction. Why don't they read their Bible?

Maybe the Devil would vomit *them* out on dry land. What did God tell Jonah to preach to Nineveh, repent or they would be destroyed they did repent, and God spared them. Several years later they became wicked again, God did not send a Jonah this time, he destroyed them completely. One should read their story from the Bible.

Nobody else will like where the Devil has them living when they find out he is nothing but a liar and cannot keep a one of his promises. God's promises go on forever, but they are not for just everybody. The Devil won't have the earth for them to live on or a body for them to live in after God tosses him and his people into a fire that burns forever. Along with the entire polluted creation. How much does one value his soul?

God says you can tell by the one he is aligning his spirit with. If we do not know God, the creator, we do not know the one we are serving. God says all honor that God does not receive, the Devil receives. If we do not know God I fail to see how we can honor him? That sounds like we are living to honor the Devil whether we know it are not. God does not bother the ones that do not love him, they are dead to him. They don't need to get in his or his people's way that are obeying God.

If one does not like this world and the things that are going on, then he had better be making some changes. Satan is running things on and of the world until God is going to burn away all evidence of it and anything that ever existed on it, except what belongs to Christ.

The Bible has made it plain as to what is going to happen. If one will study it prayerfully, one can stay ahead of Satan's grounded plan, "To Divide and Conquer, everything he possible can." Satan is not going to change his plan, maybe his tactics a little, but not his plan. It is looking like he has gotten everything of this world that is anything, divided and conquered including our once great country. Why not? We had nobody to stand in his way. It is hard to win much by voting, the devil's people almost always out numbers God's people. Only if we would preach, pray, teach a little harder maybe God will divide them up a little.

It is now talking Civil War more every day. The Devil possessed Democrats did it once and working on doing it again. Anything to divided and destroy the union and conquer it if they can abort and kill all the white kids and allow millions and millions of darker illegal aliens to flood over our borders they will have this country in their hands by vote. The Lord does not do that, it comes from the Devil we are on his property. Adam gave it to him.

They accuse us of being races, God says in Romans two; that the ones that are accusing are guilty of the same thing. I have not seen a scripture in the Bible that names the Left Politicians any plainer than that one does.

The established Republicans are backing them all they can. We each need to ask ourselves, are we one of them that is a God hating devil's child, or asleep and cannot see what is going on? If one does not know the difference in what is of Christ and what is of the Devil, he is asleep for sure, and does not know what is happening. Again, it is my intent to try to wake up a few that have got any life left in them. They are not hard to recognize.

The Word of God is the best thing I know to wake up a sleeping soul. A civil war would wake up both sides but that is a big price to pay. Look at the last one, worked really well to clean a country of people up; both sides. That is what this Book is meant to be about. It is easier to write and preach for God, than fight a war for the Devil.

There is no end of the Word of God, it is going to heaven with God's people without a change made in it, at the end of the world. Do we think we will see the end of God? The end of the world will be the beginning of Jesus Christ with us, and our new life with him.

Them that know Christ have a wonderful future to look forward to. Them that don't know him have no future but the Mystery Babylon False Prophet and the Antichrist to look to, and their future is to be tossed into the lake of fire that never quits burning. Along with the Devil, death and hell, and every soul whose name is not written down in the Lamb's Book of Life.

Some people preach if you have ever had your name written down in the Lamb's Book of Life that it can never be taken out, called once in grace always in grace. But God speaks of taking them out. I guess one can believe who one wants to believe but I choose to believe God. He is going to have the last say and I do not figure on arguing with him on one thing. I don't feel like I need to straighten Jesus out.

I have always said I do not think much of a preacher that spends more time explaining God's Word away than explaining God's Word. I believe God said what he meant to say and meant what he said, he does not need anyone to straighten him out on a thing he *meant* to say. Them kind are what God calls a double minded person and is unstable in all their ways. I can look in the rest of the Bible for at least two and three witness's other places in the Bible to establish every word like he said to do. They will be there, and they will not establish a word found in the Bible to the wrong side of what it means.

One is not established that makes up his own mind and says that is the way God meant to say it. Who is going to stand in the gap for them kind of preachers? The way is narrow but not ruff and hard, unless we make it that way. Listening to Satan and following after him will do just that. This is why we must love the Lord, or your way will be ruff.

God promises an eternity of bliss for them that will endure for him. One has nothing to lose and everything to gain, the choice is ours. That choice does not require a lot of intelligence, just some common sense. God is common sense. If one does not have him, one is not very smart. He is living on borrowed time, and must be listening to the Devil.

www.ingramcontent.com/pod-product-compliance
Lightning Source LLC
Chambersburg PA
CBHW020130130526
44591CB00032B/593